CRAZY

Easy & Proven Ways to Heal Yourself When You Feel Like Your Brain Is Broken

Darienne Garner

A Note from The Author

In my experience, there are a lot of resources out there to help people with anxiety, stress and depression. Many of them focus a great deal on why these experiences happen to some people, but seem to lack tangible, actionable things that you can actually ***do.***

I endeavored in these pages to provide simple, easy to follow ideas of steps you can implement right away, to start seeing improvement.

I am a professional counsellor, and I have been in direct practice with clients since I began my career, and a great majority of my clients arrive for their intake session claiming they suffer with anxiety and/or depression, among other things.

Although there are clinical definitions of each of many of these disorders and are included in the Diagnostic and Statistical Manual of Mental Disorders (DSM), with several different categories and diagnosis, in my experiences, many clients that I see do not have a formal diagnosis by a medical doctor or psychiatrist.

Nevertheless, my approach to working with clients is based on their own perceptions, not necessarily some label placed on them by another professional. Formal diagnosis can be useful to identify an area of need, or a specific issue that needs to be addressed, but it is not a requirement for me to try and help people.

The underlying assumption in many of my ideas and suggestions is that our perceptions shape a great deal of how we live day to day. In other words, how we think, what we think about, and what we choose to put our physical and emotional energy into will shape the course of our day, and ultimately, our life. If you focus only on what is going wrong in your life, things will appear to always go wrong. If you strive for perfection, you will consistently meet with failure. If you wait for others to change, so that your life is better, you will be waiting forever. If you consistently put others before yourself, you will never be fulfilled, content or truly happy. ***Self-care is not selfish.***

I refer to myself as a generalist. Essentially, what that means is that I do not adhere to a single theoretical perspective and approach. I draw from many theories, ideas, approaches, and perspectives to try and work with my clients to develop strategies and ideas that will work for them. I utilize strategies from Cognitive Behavioural Therapy, Dialectical Behaviour Therapy, Choice Theory, Acceptance & Commitment Therapy, just to name a few. Sometimes, I combine them, and sometimes I create or invent activities and strategies for my clients based on several them all at once.

With any self-help endeavor, I always tell my clients to "take what speaks to you and leave the rest." There will be many ideas that you find amazing and can't wait to try, and others that you will think won't work, and that's okay too. All I ask is that you give a strategy a reasonable amount of time before you decide whether it works. Researchers have shown that it takes approximately 21 days to form a new habit, so that would be a great place to start. Give a strategy 2-3 weeks of daily practice before you make a determination on its effectiveness.

Remember, without change, nothing changes. Be brave, be strong, be diligent, and I can guarantee you will feel better than you did yesterday.

Feel free to adapt any suggestions to suit your needs. This book is designed to help challenge your perceptions and move you away from negativity and to a better place.

Not only am I a professional who sees this every day in my practice, I personally also suffered with severe anxiety, recurring depression and enormous amounts of stress for as long as I can remember. So trust me when I say that I absolutely understand what these emotions feel like. I know how debilitating it can be, how much pain and sadness and inability to function comes with feeling this way.

The good news? I believe I have come out the other side of it. Although it never completely goes away, I have learned ways to cope and deal with my emotions so that I can finally be happy, healthy, and content.

You can get there too; I have faith in you.

- Darienne Garner, 2023

Table of Contents

TRIGGER WARNING:

This book is about mental health issues. It discusses various mental health conditions and symptoms, and it contains mention of sensitive topics like alcohol abuse, drug use, restrictive eating, self-harm, and suicide.

INTRODUCTION

Do you ever feel like your brain might be broken?

Do you experience overwhelming emotions that you don't understand? Are your feelings always changing, and your mood never stable? Do your own thoughts always seem to upset you? Is it a battle to get through each day? Does everything sometimes seem completely hopeless? Do you wish you could just be someone else?

Well, you are not alone. There are millions of people around the world who are affected by mental health challenges, and experience many of the same confusing and distressing struggles as you.

Living with a mental health condition can lead people to believe that their brains are broken, and that they will never be able to cope or thrive like everyone else. These unseen illnesses can be difficult for other people to understand, but they can affect every part of our lives.

The good news is that there is something you can do about it. You can actively work to manage your symptoms, and you do not have to let your mental health challenges overshadow your entire life.

It is possible for you to heal your broken brain and to live a happy and healthy life. This book is filled with a variety of practical and actionable ways in which you can help yourself to do exactly that.

A Journey to Good Mental Health

Chapter 1 focuses on what life really feels like for someone whose mental health is less than ideal. It describes the different thoughts and emotions they struggle with on a daily basis, as well as how their behaviors and relationships are negatively impacted by their mental health challenges.

Chapter 2 aims to provide brief theoretical context about mental illness. It includes an overview of different definitions, diagnoses, and treatments, and it also highlights exactly what it means to live with good mental health.

This information will be useful in giving you a greater understanding of mental health in general, but it is important to avoid self-diagnosing during this chapter. Instead, if necessary, you should seek professional assistance in obtaining a diagnosis for your unique symptoms and struggles.

Chapters 3 through 13 encompass the majority of this book, and they explore what you can do to help yourself cope and thrive on a daily basis. These chapters outline different tools and techniques for managing the symptoms of mental health conditions and dealing with various mental health challenges. The overarching goal of these strategies is to give you practical and actionable ways to help yourself.

How to Heal

Chapter 3 starts us off on our journey to healing by outlining several easy and short-term strategies for coping with overwhelming moments of stress and anxiety. These distress tolerance techniques are vital for dealing with emotional distress and for controlling harmful impulses.

Chapter 4 focuses on mindfulness as a more long-term strategy for coping with stress and for learning to live a more peaceful life. This chapter describes mindfulness skills and outlines the steps of mindful meditation. Chapter 5 continues the theme of general stress management by highlighting the importance of relaxation. It explores several different relaxation techniques designed to boost your physical and mental health.

The next chapter helps you to deal directly with your emotions. Chapter 6 examines emotional regulation techniques in order to teach you to better understand and control your own feelings. The goal of this chapter is for you to gain greater insight, resilience, and stability. Chapter 7 has a similar aim in helping you to address your own thoughts. This chapter provides practical tools for countering negative thoughts and cognitive distortions.

Chapter 8 moves us on to the behavioral section of this book with its exploration of journaling as a mental health tool. This chapter sets out different journaling strategies for self-reflection and self-monitoring. Chapter 9 furthers this latter concept by focusing on the importance of living with intention, motivation, and purpose. It outlines practical tools for how to live more deliberately, such as activity scheduling, behavior activation, and goal setting. Chapter 10 provides a guide for problem-solving to help you maximize the benefits of other techniques.

Chapter 11 aims to bring these tools together by examining the related concept of self-esteem. It explores practical ways of building your confidence and using positivity to improve how you see yourself.

Chapter 12 is dedicated to relationships, and it examines tools for interpersonal effectiveness. This chapter highlights the importance of social interaction, and it provides practical techniques for improving your communication and interpersonal skills.

The final chapter of this book returns to our relationship with ourselves. Chapter 13 looks at self-care tools and techniques, and it ends off our journey with an important message: You are worthy and capable of living well.

CHAPTER 1: FEELING BROKEN

There are many different assumptions about mental health issues, so it can be difficult to understand exactly what it means to be mentally ill. Moreover, if you do not personally have a mental health condition, it can be hard to grasp what it really feels like to live with one.

Mental illness is not as neat and clear cut as having a specific diagnosis and set of symptoms. It is not always as simple as people would assume, and treating a mental health condition is far more unique and complex than most people realize.

In reality, having a mental health condition means dealing with a vast range of complicated and contradictory thoughts and emotions. It can mean living each day frustrated and hopeless, and constantly wishing that you could think and behave differently. Mental illness is about feeling that your brain is irreparably broken, and believing that you will never be able to cope and thrive like everyone else.

This chapter aims to explain more about how it actually feels for the person whose mental health is less than ideal, and its goal is to create an accurate and empathetic picture of daily experiences and struggles. It will also provide some essential hope to hang on to: If you are suffering from a mental health condition, know that you are not alone, and you are not helpless.

What It's Really Like

Thoughts and Feelings

If you are living with mental health challenges, you will be intimately familiar with what an intense emotional experience this can be. Not only are your emotions often too extreme or inappropriate for the situation, but they can also be infuriatingly inconsistent.

You do not know what it means to have mood stability: One minute, you can be feeling down and depressed, but then the next minute, you start to feel manic and impulsive for no reason. Or, perhaps you become angry out of nowhere, and are suddenly filled with a confusing rage that frightens you. You also regularly feel afraid and anxious, even when there is nothing apparently wrong. Ultimately, living with mental health struggles can mean that you never know how you might feel or how long you will feel that way.

What you do know is that stress will be your constant companion. If you suffer from a mental health condition, you will know what it feels like to worry and overthink until you have exhausted yourself. You regularly go around in circles in your own head, and you stress so much that you can never eat or sleep properly. You often feel frozen by your anxiety, and you rarely manage to get yourself out of this cycle.

You also struggle with your opinion of yourself. You suffer from low self-esteem, but you are constantly changing how you see yourself. You vacillate between worrying that you are a bad person and not even knowing who you are. You never know what you want or what you believe, but you do know that you are ashamed of how you feel.

Mostly, you are terrified that people will find out that you are mentally ill.

Problematic Behavior

Having a mental health condition can also mean struggling on a daily basis with what seem like ordinary and easy tasks. You battle to find the motivation and energy for simple things, and you often berate yourself for not coping like everyone else. Moreover, your mental health condition can mean that you are not able to take good care of yourself, or that you do not even want to. Your physical health and hygiene go down the drain, which only worsens how you feel about yourself and your life.

You start to hate yourself because you think that if you're not perfect then you are worthless. You find that you either try too hard or you give up entirely, even though you are chronically afraid of failure. You aren't able to work like you used to because you can't concentrate or motivate yourself. You then feel guilty for not trying hard enough, and you become obsessed with the idea that everything will be okay if you just try harder.

At the same time, however, you begin to lose interest in your life completely. You no longer do the things that you used to enjoy, and you don't even care that you've stopped doing them. You just can't be bothered, and while you are mostly bored and numb, you also panic about the state of things: You worry that you will never enjoy life again, and that you will never be happy.

People who live with mental illness will also know how common it is to struggle with self-destructive and self-sabotaging behavior. You battle with addictions like spending more than you have, drinking too much, or sleeping with people impulsively. You hate that these vices control you, but you are also desperate for a way of getting out of your own head. You know that you are only making things worse, but you can't get yourself to let go of your crutches.

Relationship Trouble

Mental health conditions do not just affect what is going on in your head and how you behave. Unfortunately, they seep into all aspects of your life, and begin to affect your relationships with others.

Mental illness can cause you to isolate yourself from those around you because you just don't have the energy, empathy, or enthusiasm to deal with people. You get irritable and defensive when loved ones try to help: You lash out, and then regret it later. You know that they only want what's best for you, but you are also suspicious that they just pity you and find you pathetic.

Similarly, you worry constantly about what people think, and you assume that they are always judging you negatively. It is common to catch yourself comparing your life to everyone else's, and you get frustrated because other people seem to have it so easy. You feel like life is harder and more stressful for you, but you can't seem to understand why that would be the case.

Above all, you are plagued by the belief that you are a burden, and that everyone you love will leave. And so, you push people away to avoid rejection—only to feel lonely and desperate for their love and attention soon after.

Helpless and Hopeless

Ultimately, mental illness is about struggling with instability, distress, and pain in all areas of your life. It is about frustration, contradiction, self-hatred, and confusion, among many other things.

Mental health challenges can mean that you are often in extreme emotional pain, so much so that you frequently think about self-harm and suicide. You are aware that you need help with your condition and its symptoms, but you are ashamed that you can't just "suck it up." You also want to get help, but are pretty sure that you are beyond all hope anyway. You worry about having to be medicated to function, and you resent having to choose between feeling "crazy" and being numb.

You feel like life is meaningless, and you are constantly searching for something. You are never satisfied, fulfilled, or happy—you are always looking for something more. Above all, while you are convinced that the world is better off without you, you don't know why or how to change.

The Good News

If you find yourself identifying with any of the above, or are worried that your loved one might, then keep reading because there is good news to come. Even though you may feel broken and helpless, the next section will cover two important messages of hope:

- Millions of people feel the way you do, and you are not alone in your mental health challenges.

- It is entirely possible to live a full, happy, and healthy life, despite your mental health condition.

You Are Not Alone

Millions of people around the world suffer from mental illness, which means that they think, feel, and behave in much the same way you do.

In fact, 1 in 5 adults in America are currently living with a mental illness, which is over 50 million people in this one country alone (Anonymous, 2023). Globally, 1 in 8 people suffer from a mental health disorder, and this statistic translates to 970 million people worldwide (Anonymous, 2022). Moreover, each year, 1 in 25 people are classified as having a mental illness serious enough to cause significant impairment in their daily functioning (Holland, 2023).

Depending on your unique situation, it may also be helpful for you to know some other contextual factors about mental illness:

- Women are more likely than men to suffer from a mental health condition.
- Those in the age range of 18 to 25 years are the most likely to see an onset of mental illness.
- People from mixed race backgrounds are more at risk than those of a single race background for developing a mental illness.

As you work through the tools of this book, hold on to all of this knowledge as motivation that you are not alone in your struggles and effort.

A Happy and Healthy Life

Another crucial piece of hope to keep close is the fact that your mental health challenges do not have to stop you from living a full and happy life. Your mental health condition does not have to define who you are, and its symptoms do not have to control your everyday emotions and behaviors.

While your mental illness may not be curable, there are many techniques that you can use to reduce and manage your symptoms. This book contains a wealth of strategies that you can actively employ on a daily basis, and its chapters are filled with actionable tools for addressing your thoughts, emotions, and behaviors.

The strategies of this book are aimed at helping you to reach your full potential in different ways, and they will put you firmly on the path to good mental health. Ultimately, as you learn each new tool, keep in mind that you have a lot of power to make your mental health struggles manageable, and that you can thrive in spite of your condition.

CHAPTER 2: MENTAL HEALTH 101

As we learned in Chapter 1, millions of people around the world are affected by mental health challenges. Many struggle on a daily basis with the symptoms of their condition, but often they do not fully understand their unseen illness. Moreover, there are many misconceptions about what it means to have good mental health.

As such, this chapter will delve more deeply into ideas around mental illness and mental health. It will explore different definitions and types of mental health disorders, describe common signs and symptoms, and look at traditionally accepted treatments and therapies.

Ultimately, the most important thing to understand about good mental health is that it is not simply the absence of mental illness. Rather, having good mental health is about developing positive characteristics like emotional resilience and a sense of purpose.

What Is Mental Illness?

Mental illness is a broad term that encompasses hundreds of different conditions that affect the way someone feels, thinks, and behaves. From a clinical and medical perspective, a mental health disorder is defined as any illness that causes significant disturbance to a person's behavior, cognitive functioning, and emotional regulation. The origin of these conditions can be derived from a range of factors, and it is important to remember that anyone can experience mental health struggles.

Mental illness can be caused by biological factors related to brain structure, brain chemistry, and genetics. It is possible for someone to inherit a psychological predisposition to a certain condition, but mental illness can also be the result of traumatic or abusive experiences during the developmental stages of childhood. Moreover, a person can experience a decline in their mental health later in life due to environmental factors like violence, poverty, and inequality.

Spotting the Signs

On that note, there are several common signs and symptoms that can be helpful in indicating a general decline in your mental health:

- You begin to overeat or eat too little.
- You struggle with insomnia, or find yourself sleeping more than usual.
- You feel fatigued even when you have had enough sleep.
- You experience unexplainable body pains.
- You suffer from extreme mood swings.
- You often experience feelings of numbness, hopelessness, or helplessness.

- You struggle with other emotions like confusion, forgetfulness, irritability, anger, anxiety, sadness, or fearfulness.
- You engage in activities like smoking, drinking, or using drugs more than ever before.
- You distance yourself from loved ones.
- You lose interest in your favorite activities.
- You are unable to complete daily tasks and chores.
- You see or hear things that aren't there.
- You genuinely believe things that aren't consistent with reality.
- You experience frequent thoughts of self-harm and suicide.

Different Types of Disorders

Ultimately, there are many different categories of mental health conditions: depression, bipolar, anxiety disorders, eating disorders, obsessive compulsive disorders (OCD), post-traumatic stress disorder (PTSD), schizophrenia, and schizotypal disorders.

A broad distinction is often made between mood disorders and personality disorders, and this categorization can be useful for understanding how different types of mental health struggles overlap and relate.

Mood Disorders

Mood disorders are mental health conditions that are characterized by a person's thought patterns, energy levels, and ability to regulate their emotions.

Depression

Depression is a common and well-known example of a mood disorder. In 2019, 280 million people around the world reported suffering from a form of depression (Anonymous, 2022). The different types of depression include major depression, seasonal affective disorder, and persistent depressive disorder, and many of the symptoms of these subtypes are related.

During a depressive episode, a person will experience a depressed mood, which means that they feel empty, sad, irritable, helpless, and hopeless. They may also struggle with energy and concentration, and experience difficulty sleeping, eating, and functioning as they normally do. Depression can also cause overwhelming feelings of guilt, low self-worth, and despondency about the future. Moreover, someone suffering from depression may be plagued by thoughts of self-harm or suicide.

Anxiety

Anxiety is another mood disorder that affects millions of people each year. Anxiety disorders are actually the most common mental health conditions, with 301 million people suffering from a type of anxiety in 2019 (Anonymous, 2022). As with depression, there are different kinds of anxiety disorders: generalized anxiety disorder, social anxiety disorder, phobias, and separation anxiety disorder.

All anxiety disorders are defined by feelings of excessive worry and fear that cause the sufferer to experience behavioral and emotional distress. For example, those who struggle with social anxiety disorder are incredibly fearful of social interaction, and so they have difficulty meeting new people, socializing, and maintaining interpersonal relationships. Someone with generalized anxiety will find themselves struggling to function on a daily basis because they are consumed by irrational worries, fears, and nervousness.

Personality Disorders

Personality disorders are conditions that affect a person's perception of themselves and those around them, as well as how they approach interpersonal relationships. In clinical terms, personality disorders are characterized by enduring patterns of inner experiences and interpersonal behavior that are at odds with societal expectations and cultural norms.

This category of mental health conditions includes antisocial personality disorder, narcissistic personality disorder, avoidant personality disorder, and paranoid personality disorder. These conditions can be biological or genetic in origin, but it is more commonly thought that they develop as a result of problematic relationships or traumatic experiences during a person's childhood development.

Borderline Personality Disorder

Borderline personality disorder (BPD) is one of the most common personality disorders. Its defining characteristic is instability in various aspects of a person's life: their mood, self-image, behavior, relationships, and functioning.

Those who suffer from BPD experience intense and fluctuating emotions, and they struggle with impulsivity and inflexible thinking. Many people with BPD will go to extremes in order to avoid abandonment, and they are generally drawn to risky and self-destructive behavior. Above all, BPD causes someone to have an unstable sense of self, which leads to a lot of distress and confusion for the sufferer.

Treating Mental Illness

If you find yourself identifying with any of the symptoms or conditions described above, the most important first step is to seek professional guidance. Avoid trying to self-diagnose your mental health condition, and rather, speak with a medical professional about your symptoms and struggles. You can start by visiting your primary care doctor who will conduct a physical exam and mental health screening. They can then create an action plan for your treatment, or refer you on to a psychologist or psychiatrist if need be.

While there is no one-size-fits-all treatment for mental illness, traditional treatment plans include medication, therapy, or a combination of both. The primary aim of treating mental health conditions is not to cure them, but rather, to address their underlying causes and manage their symptoms.

In terms of medication, a general practitioner or psychiatrist could recommend and prescribe medication that falls into one of several categories: antidepressants, anti-psychotics, anti-anxiety medications, and mood stabilizers. From a therapy perspective, two of the most common approaches a therapist or psychologist will take are cognitive behavioral therapy (CBT) and dialectical behavior therapy (DBT).

Cognitive Behavioral Therapy

CBT is a type of therapy that examines the relationship between thoughts, emotions, and behaviors. The aim is to investigate how unhealthy thought patterns and core beliefs can lead to self-destructive and harmful behaviors. In this way, CBT combines behavioral theory, which emphasizes the role of learning in developing behaviors, and cognitive therapy, which focuses on dysfunctional thinking patterns.

The end goal of CBT is to help people find more positive ways of thinking in order to create more constructive beliefs and behaviors. The patient should also develop a deeper understanding of themselves and why they think, feel, and behave the way they do.

Dialectical Behavior Therapy

DBT was first developed as a therapy for those suffering from BPD as a way of treating their self-harm and suicidal impulses.

The main aims of the DBT are to help people regulate their emotions and tolerate distress. The end goals of these modules are to learn impulse control and to develop the ability to deal with harmful thoughts and emotions in constructive ways. DBT also has techniques centered on becoming more mindful and improving interpersonal relationships.

Ultimately, the word "dialectical" fully captures the foundation of this treatment philosophy: Those who undergo this therapy should emerge with a better capacity to deal with the existence of opposites, contradiction, and change. Patients should work to create a life that is unique to them, and that they can feel good about.

The Light at the End of the Tunnel

Many of the techniques and tools described in the rest of this book are drawn from CBT and DBT strategies. The most important takeaway, however, is not the detail of the theory and philosophy, but rather, the overall end goal that should be at the forefront of your mind: achieving good mental health.

Good mental health is not simply the absence of mental illness. As we have seen, mental health struggles are complex and diverse, and treating these conditions is centered on symptom management—learning to live and thrive despite your challenges.

In this sense, good mental health is the ability to lead a relatively happy, healthy, and stable life. It is about developing your own psychological and emotional well-being, and cultivating a set of positive characteristics in your life and within yourself.

As you apply the strategies of this book, you should notice yourself developing the following traits of good mental health:

- You feel content about your life.
- You have the ability to laugh and enjoy yourself.
- You have a passion and zeal for being.

- You live with a sense of purpose and meaning.
- You can find balance between work and play.
- You are able to employ moderation when necessary.
- You remember to allow yourself rest.
- You can maintain healthy and fulfilling relationships.

In addition to these characteristics, perhaps the most significant and defining feature of good mental health is the presence of emotional resilience.

Resilience

Resilience is the ability to cope with life's challenges, adversities, and ups and downs. It is the capacity to experience hardship and distress, and to move through these difficult moments with a positive outlook.

Resilience is about remaining flexible and adaptive during stressful times, and dealing with emotional challenges without resorting to self-sabotage. It is about developing the tools to bounce back after a disappointment or loss, and becoming undaunted by change, uncertainty, and new experiences.

Ultimately, having good mental health does not mean that you are never sad, stressed, or depressed, or that you are cured of your mental health condition. It means that you have the resilience to cope with your emotions and symptoms, and to live a happy and healthy life regardless.

CHAPTER 3: TOLERATING DISTRESS

The previous chapters highlighted that, while there are many kinds of mental health challenges, what is common across different conditions is the emotional distress experienced by sufferers.

Whether someone is struggling with depression, OCD, or an anxiety disorder, they will likely be familiar with the moments of overwhelming panic and pain caused by having mental health struggles. Moreover, what can make these moments worse are the harmful behaviors that some people use to cope with their emotions.

Ultimately, these moments—and their consequences—can be incredibly debilitating, so learning to tolerate distress constructively is a crucial place to start with our practical tools and techniques. As this chapter will show, there are a variety of simple strategies that can be implemented to help you manage emotional crises and control self-destructive impulses.

Controlling Impulses

People who live with mental health challenges regularly experience overwhelming moments of extreme emotion. They can go through periods of significant distress as a result of their mental health condition, and as such, they often struggle to feel in control of their lives.

To make matters worse, many people have developed harmful coping mechanisms for dealing with their distress. These negative strategies are often self-destructive habits: drug use, alcohol abuse, excessive spending, restrictive eating, risky sex, and self-harm.

Regardless of the specific type of behavior, the goal is usually to find immediate relief—to block out feelings of sadness, shame, and confusion, and to regain a sense of control. Over time, however, as these behaviors are consistently relied upon, they become reinforced as compulsions and impulses. This means that, in the next moment of distress, not only does the sufferer not know how else to deal with their emotions, but they are also actively drawn toward their harmful behaviors.

The Problem With Temporary Relief

There is, unfortunately, more bad news: Any relief or comfort provided by these behaviors is temporary. The situation causing the distress is not resolved through any of these avoidance tactics, and the feelings you are trying to escape will eventually return in full force. Moreover, these negative coping mechanisms are not sustainable. In the end, giving in to self-destructive impulses almost always ends up making the situation worse, and they only cause more physical and emotional harm.

Given all of this, it is vitally important to learn alternative and constructive ways of tolerating distress. Distress tolerance is about developing the ability to manage and survive an emotional crisis without feeling overwhelmed or making the situation worse. It is about accepting the reality of the situation, and learning to work through your emotions instead of trying to avoid them.

Distress tolerance involves a variety of short-term coping techniques to help people feel in control of themselves and their emotions. If implemented consistently in times of distress, you will be able to train your body and mind to respond to these techniques by returning you to emotional equilibrium after a stressor.

For example, the first technique that we will explore uses temperature, intense exercise, paced breathing, and paired muscle relaxation (TIPP) to help you calm yourself down in a moment of panic.

TIPP

The TIPP tool works by resetting and restarting the limbic system, which is the part of the brain that sends our bodies into fight or flight mode in response to stress. TIPP aims to alleviate our state of arousal, and to regulate our emotional and behavioral responses.

The TIPP strategies are simple, and easy to implement at any time and in any place. They will work within a few minutes, and you don't need anything but yourself to put them into practice.

Temperature

This first tool of TIPP is about using temperature to shock and reset your panicking system.

For example, the next time you are feeling overwhelmed, try splashing your face with cold water. You can also take a relatively cold shower, or even try holding ice cubes in your hands.

Intense Exercise

The aim of the second TIPP strategy is to manipulate your own biochemistry, and to bring yourself down naturally from a stressful high through intense exercise.

One way of doing this is by going for a quick, short run the next time you are feeling distressed. You can also try other high intensity cardio exercises like jumping jacks, skipping, or high knees.

The aim is to get your blood pumping and your heart racing. The adrenaline coursing through your body will bring you to a state of physical and mental euphoria. You can then rest as you normally would after exercise, and your body will naturally start to calm its own systems.

Paced Breathing

The first "P" in TIPP refers to a breathing exercise called paced breathing. The aim of this tool is to bring control to your panicking body and mind by regulating your breathing and lowering your heart rate and blood pressure.

Paced breathing is simple and easy to practice in the moment: Inhale through your nose for two seconds, hold your breath for three, and then exhale slowly out your mouth for five seconds. Repeat this process until you feel you have calmed down sufficiently.

Paired Muscle Relaxation

The second "P" in TIPP is often overlooked, but it is another easy way to use the connection between your mind and body. The aim of paired muscle relaxation is to relax your body physically in order to emotionally calm your mind.

To practice this technique, start by focusing on the muscles in the toes. Tense these muscles simultaneously as you breathe in, and then relax them together as you breathe out. Move on to focus on the next pair of muscles, and do the same. Work your way up your body slowly and progressively until you reach your facial muscles.

Self-Soothe

Self-soothing is another useful distress tolerance technique. This tool is about being able to comfort yourself when you are feeling overwhelmed. It involves picking an item, activity, or behavior that can act as an emotional security blanket, and using these tools to calm yourself down.

Think back to when you were a young child and how you would cling to your favorite toy, or even suck your thumb, when you were scared or confused. The theory behind the self-soothing technique is the same. Of course, as an adult, it's important to find a developmentally appropriate means of comfort. Everyone's self-soothing strategies will be unique, and your main priority is simply to focus on what works best for you.

In making this decision, it is also crucial to be aware of what might be personally problematic. Many people will drink a glass of wine or eat a chocolate bar as a means of comforting themselves, but if you are someone who struggles with alcohol abuse or emotional eating, these will not be healthy options for you.

A Box of Comfort

It can be really helpful to have your chosen self-soothing tools nearby and ready to go when they are needed. You can make sure of this by setting up a self-soothing toolkit. This is a box or drawer where you keep your security blanket items so that they are right within reach during moments of panic.

When preparing your comfort box, try to incorporate items that will engage all of your senses. This will allow you to ground yourself physically and emotionally, and there are several ways to ensure that you incorporate all five senses:

- Stock your box with tasty snacks and treats.
- Be sure to add in smelly oils, candles, and lotions.
- Try to include a few cozy and tactile blankets and sweaters.
- Make sure to keep guided meditations and playlists of your favorite songs.
- Fill the space with visual reminders of your loved ones like photos, trinkets, and memorabilia.

Improving the Moment

In addition to calming and comforting yourself, you can also cope with an overwhelming situation by learning how to change your perception of it. This involves using the distress tolerance tools like imagery, meaning, prayer, relaxation, one thing at a time, vacation, and encouragement (IMPROVE).

The aim of the IMPROVE tool is to provide you with practical strategies for changing your perception in order to make your distress more manageable.

Imagery

The imagery tool of IMPROVE is about visualization. It involves imagining a different situation than the stressful one you are currently facing. The idea is to escape briefly to an alternate reality by visualizing something more peaceful in your mind.

It is important to fully immerse yourself in your fantasy by engaging all of your senses. This means playing out a scenario in which you can see, hear, taste, touch, and smell different things. For more guidance on how to create these fantasies, jump ahead to Chapter 5 and its section on using visualization as a relaxation technique.

Meaning

The "M" in the IMPROVE strategy is about finding meaning in a stressful event in order to make the situation easier to cope with. The idea of this tool is to find a more positive way of shaping a stressor, and to give yourself a sense of purpose when facing a crisis.

As such, the meaning tool will not only help you to shift your perception, but it will also ensure that you have more motivation when addressing a problem.

Prayer

The prayer tool of IMPROVE does not have to refer to a religious prayer, although it definitely can. The focus of this strategy is to find a mantra, quote, or saying that has meaning to you. Maybe it's something that someone once said to you that provided you with comfort, or perhaps it is a spiritual or religious prayer or passage that helps to calm you.

Once you have found your unique devotion, you can then employ it in times of stress by repeating it to yourself throughout the crisis.

Relax

The "R" in IMPROVE is about relaxation, and it can include a variety of breathing, relaxation, and stress reduction techniques. You can use the paired muscle relaxation tool or the paced breathing strategy from TIPP, or you can skip ahead to Chapter 5 for other stress reduction techniques.

Whichever technique you choose, keep in mind that your overall goal should be to calm your emotional state by physically relaxing your body.

One Thing at a Time

This technique is about slowing down and dealing with the situation one step at a time. It involves breaking up the stressful event into separate parts so that it feels less overwhelming. You can then address one part of the problem at a time before moving on to another aspect of the situation.

For more detail, have a look at the section on successive approximation in Chapter 11.

Vacation

The vacation tool is similar to the imagery technique explained above in that it is about taking a break from the stressor, both mentally and emotionally. It involves "going on a holiday" from your thoughts and emotions, and distancing yourself from the stressful situation. The idea is to take a calming and peaceful break, and then to return to face the problem head on with more energy and confidence.

The section below on distraction has some useful examples for how to remove yourself from the reality of your problem.

Encouragement

The final tool of IMPROVE is about employing positivity and self-compassion. Chapter 11 deals more fully with the value of these concepts, but in terms of distress tolerance, the focus of encouragement should be on reminding yourself that your extreme emotions will not last forever.

Specifically, this technique involves reminding yourself to be patient, and engaging in positive self-talk. This can mean practicing daily affirmations, or simply helping yourself to persevere with little reminders: everything passes, nothing lasts forever, and things will get better.

Weighing the Pros and Cons

Weighing the pros and cons is a distress tolerance technique that aims to get you out of a stressful situation by ensuring that you make a wise and rational decision.

The usefulness of this tool is in how it prevents you from making rash and impulsive decisions, and how it trains you to ignore your fight and flight impulse. Instead, this technique forces you to press pause until you have logically considered your next step.

To practice this tool in your next moment of panic, start by finding a quiet place alone to gather your thoughts. Grab a piece of paper or your journal, and write down a list of the pros and cons related to the potential actions you could take. If you prefer to verbalize your anxieties, then brainstorm your pros and cons out loud. You can speak to the wall, a close friend, or just to yourself.

Ultimately, you just need to focus on rationally considering your next move. While you are busy engaging logically with the problem, you will find that your emotional state quickly calms down. Not only will you then feel less overwhelmed, but you will now be even more capable of making a wise choice.

Distraction

Distraction is a distress tolerance technique that aims to get you focused on something other than the situation that is causing you distress. We all like to think that we can multitask, but our working memory actually has finite limits. By using distraction to overload our capacity to concentrate and remember, we can essentially get our brains to "forget" about the original stressor.

Distraction techniques are unique to each individual, and you should focus on finding an activity that works best to distract you from your emotions and thoughts. Once you have determined your ideal distraction, try using this tool in your next moment of distress. You can then return to the problem once you have had enough time to calm down, and are able to cope with the situation constructively.

It's a good idea to make sure that your chosen distractions are easy to implement, uncomplicated, and something that you can do on any ordinary day. You should also try to choose activities that demand your full attention and focus:

- Visit with a family member.
- Watch a movie at home.
- Call a friend to chat.
- Play a board game.
- Go to the gym.
- Read a book.
- Cook a meal.
- Listen to a podcast.
- Run a few errands.

- Clean the house.
- Go for a drive.

Radical Acceptance

When all else fails, just let it go. Radical acceptance is a distress tolerance technique that requires a lot of practice, but it is particularly useful when you find that other strategies are not working.

Radical acceptance is about totally relinquishing your control, and simply accepting things as they are. It involves acknowledging that some things are not within your ability to control, and that fixating on these problems will only cause more distress. Radical acceptance teaches you to unstick yourself emotionally, and to let go of your responsibility to fix a problem.

It Is What It Is

To practice radical acceptance, start by observing the situation objectively and without emotion. Determine for yourself whether this particular situation is within your control. If there is nothing that you can do to change the facts or the outcome, then simply accept this as your new reality, and move on.

Of course, this is much easier said than done, which is why radical acceptance requires so much practice. One way of helping yourself to let go is to embrace a useful mantra: It is what it is. When implementing this tool, remember to explore what this phrase means to your situation, and continue to repeat it to yourself until the pressure to fix things eventually subsides.

CHAPTER 4: MINDFULNESS

Chapter 3 focused on short-term tools for tolerating distress, which can be incredibly helpful in overwhelming moments. It is also important, however, to develop more long-term strategies for dealing with your stress and anxiety. Not only will this help you to make your mental health challenges more manageable, but it will also set you firmly on the path to good mental health. Ultimately, you want to be able to live a stable and secure life in the face of everyday obstacles and ups and downs.

Mindfulness is one essential skill for managing your stress and anxiety, and for moving toward a more peaceful life in the long term. It also has the added benefit of helping you to learn more about yourself—who you are and what you want.

The Importance of Being Present

Mindfulness is the practice of being present. It is about learning to live in the moment with intention and observance. The goal of mindfulness is to get you to pay more attention to your experience of your external environment, as well as to your internal world of thoughts and emotions.

This practice will help to develop your emotional resilience in response to stressors, and it will allow you to stay calm and logical in the face of challenges. There are also several other benefits to the practice of mindfulness:

- It helps you to stop fixating on the past.
- It allows you to stop worrying about the future.
- It enables you to learn more about yourself, your character, and your goals.
- It helps you to control your emotions and thoughts.

We all naturally possess the ability to be mindful, but deliberately practicing mindfulness skills will make them easier to access in times of stress.

"What" Skills

Mindfulness can be practiced anywhere and at any time. While you will need to engage with these skills intentionally at the start of your journey, your overall goal should be to cultivate an awareness mindset. Eventually, you want mindfulness to be a way of living that comes naturally to you.

For beginners, the practice of mindfulness is easily divided into two sets of skills: "what" skills and "how" skills. "What" skills are the practical actions you can engage in to develop your mindfulness, and "how" skills refer to the manner in which you must practice these actions.

Observing

Observation is the first ""what" mindfulness skill that you can practice. This skill is about simply paying attention. The goal is to notice things about your life more intentionally, and to become generally more aware of yourself and your surroundings.

Practice this skill by just observing what is going on around you. You want to bring yourself consciously to the present moment by noticing the environment you are in, as well as how you are feeling physically and emotionally.

A good trick to kick-start your observing is to engage all of your senses: Ask yourself what you can see, hear, smell, taste, and touch in the present moment.

At the beginning of your mindfulness journey, you might want to set aside 10 or 15 minutes during which you can intentionally practice your observation skills. Over time, however, you should find yourself observing naturally throughout your day.

Describing

The next "what" skill builds on your observation practice. For step two of mindfulness, you need to start adding words to describe what you have been observing. This often happens unconsciously as you observe, but you can make your mindfulness practice more concrete and specific if you intentionally describe your experience.

Initially, it might help to verbalize your descriptions literally. Saying these things out loud to yourself may seem silly at first, but it will really help you to practice identifying and naming your observations.

This conscious effort will get you closer to the end goal of mindfulness—to live intentionally in the moment—and, over time, the words will come more naturally.

Participating

In this modern day, it is very easy to get busy and distracted. It seems as though there are never-ending demands on our attention: invasive social media, 24-7 news cycles, the pressure of productivity, the need to multitask, and the fear of missing out. All of these factors escalate our anxiety and stress, and mindfulness forces us to slow down for our own good.

The final "what" skill does this by encouraging us to be more conscious and deliberate in our everyday tasks and activities. The participating skill is about engaging fully in whatever you are doing, and staying present in that one moment.

For example, if you are reading a book, your aim should be to participate deliberately in this task by giving it your undivided attention. This means not picking up your phone every few minutes to check your messages, or putting on a TV series in the background.

Overall, participating is about breaking your multitasking habits, and learning to devote your full attention to an activity. This skill will take practice, but you can quite literally practice it in whatever you do each day.

“How” Skills

The “how” skills set out the manner in which you should practice mindfulness actions. They serve as a practical guide for how you should be observing, describing, and participating.

Nonjudgmental

When engaging in mindfulness, it is crucial that you reduce all judgment. It is natural for us to want to categorize and label something as either good or bad, but the goal of mindfulness is simply to recognize things as they are.

As such, it is very important to avoid making any moral judgments or assumptions about your observations, descriptions, or participation practice.

For example, you might observe that it is a cloudy day, but be careful not to insert a moral judgment: A cloudy day is bad because it means that it might rain, and you hate the rain. Instead, simply note that it is cloudy, or passively observe that it might rain, and reserve any further inferences.

Similarly, if you are trying to participate fully in a task but find yourself getting distracted, don’t get frustrated with your inattention. Instead of chastising and berating yourself, remain neutral, simply notice that you have lost focus, and return to concentrating on your chosen activity.

One Mindful

"One mindfulness" is about being in one mind when observing, describing, and participating. This simply means taking everything one step at a time, and focusing on one thing at a time.

For example, if you are feeling overwhelmed by your environment, try to deal with just one thing: Observe one aspect of your surroundings, or note just one emotion you are having. You can then describe it fully for yourself before moving on to another aspect.

The participating skill is also a great way to practice living one mindfully. As we have seen, it requires that you engage fully in one moment or activity.

Effective

The final "how" skill is about doing whatever works best for you. Effectiveness means focusing on the things that serve you, and learning to let go of those that do not.

With this skill, it is important not to worry about what you think you should be doing, or about being right. You should not be too concerned with what other people might think, and rather, put yourself first if that is what is most effective.

For example, holding on to grudges, even when you have been genuinely wronged, is only going to make you resentful and bitter. Instead, try to let go of these things that no longer serve your best interest.

You can incorporate effectiveness into your mindfulness practice by observing, describing, and participating in whatever is best for you. Try to notice these things about yourself, and practice focusing on what adds to your life.

Structured Mindfulness Practices

The “what” and “how” skills explained above can be practiced anytime, anywhere, and however you like. There are also many structured mindfulness exercises that can be useful in providing guidance at the start of your practice.

Note that you will need to set aside time in your day—around 30 minutes—to participate in these practices. Try to make a solid commitment to yourself about when, where, and how you will engage in these techniques.

Grounding

Grounding techniques are really effective ways of bringing yourself to the present moment physically and emotionally. The 5-4-3-2-1 grounding technique is particularly useful as a mindfulness practice because it engages all of your senses.

This technique is easy and simple to implement. Start by taking a look at your immediate surroundings, and ground yourself through observation and description:

1. Notice five things that you can see, and describe these things for yourself.

2. Identify and describe four things that you can feel with your physical touch.
3. Focus on and describe three things that you can hear.
4. Notice and describe two things that you can smell.
5. Bring awareness to your final sense, and describe one thing that you can taste.

This grounding exercise can be used on its own as a mindfulness practice, but it is also a great foundational tool to use before moving on to a more in-depth mindful meditation.

Seated Meditation

One structured form of mindfulness meditation is seated meditation. This exercise encourages you to set aside time for mindfulness, and its steps are simple and easy to implement:

1. Start by finding a quiet room or a place where you won't be disturbed.
2. Sit down on the floor in whatever position is most comfortable for you. Try to keep your posture straight, but most importantly, remain relaxed.
3. Close your eyes, and breathe slowly in and out of your nose until you feel settled.
4. Bring yourself to focus on the present moment through observation: Observe any physical sensations, notice the

aspects of the external environment, and pay attention to your emotions and thoughts.

5. Note that your head is not going to become an empty vacuum. You will still have distracting thoughts and emotions, but remember to engage nonjudgmentally with these intrusions: notice them, accept them, and let them pass on by.

6. Continue your nonjudgmental observation for a set amount of time. Start by aiming for 10 minutes, and have an end goal of working up to 30 minutes of seated meditation each day.

Walking Meditation

Walking meditation is another deliberate and structured mindfulness practice. It is a more active and energized way of observing, describing, and participating:

1. Find a quiet road or pathway around 20 feet in length. Avoid busy paths and parks as these can prove very distracting.

2. Start walking slowly back and forth along your chosen path.

3. Try to keep your stride, arm movement, and breathing consistent and regular.

4. Once you feel settled into a rhythm, turn your attention to observation. Start by focusing intently on the physical sensation of walking: Notice how your feet feel touching the ground, how your muscles tense as you move, and how your arms feel swinging by your side.

5. Broaden your observations to the environment around you: Observe and describe the pathway, the weather, and the time of day.

6. Then turn to observing your own emotions and thoughts as you walk. Remember to be nonjudgmental and one mindful in addressing your inner world.

7. Continue this walking meditation for 20 to 30 minutes. Consider setting a timer on your watch or phone that will let you know when your meditation session is over.

Body Scan Meditation

This final mindful meditation exercise is centered on observing your own body, and bringing yourself into the present moment through physical sensation:

1. Start by finding a quiet place. Choose a spot with comfortable flooring, or bring along a blanket or exercise mat.

2. Lie down on your back, extend your arms and legs out straight on the floor, and turn your palms to face upward.

3. Breathe slowly in and out of your nose, or conduct a grounding exercise in order to settle yourself into the moment.

4. Start to zone in your attention: Focus on your toes first, and observe their physical sensations. Try wriggling them to draw your attention. Describe for yourself what you are feeling as you become more aware of this body part.

5. Move on to focus on your feet, and determine how they feel. Scan them for physical sensation, and notice if they are itchy, tingling, sore, numb, and so on.

6. Move up your body progressively, and focus your attention on each next body part deliberately: your calves, knees, thighs, buttocks, stomach, chest, arms, hands, and head.

7. For each body part, take note of any physical sensations, and remember to be nonjudgmental and one mindful in observing any related thoughts or emotions that you may have.

8. Once you have moved through and scanned your entire body, your practice is complete.

CHAPTER 5: RELAXATION TECHNIQUES

In addition to the mindfulness skills and practices of Chapter 4, there are many other simple relaxation techniques that you can use to manage your stress and reduce your anxiety.

Learning to relax your body is important for coping with the stress of your mental health challenges, and for moving toward the end goal of good mental health. There are also several other physical and emotional benefits to triggering the body's relaxation response: lower blood pressure, improved sleep, increased focus and concentration, and a boosted mood.

As you work through this chapter, keep in mind that these techniques take practice. It is important that you give yourself time to recognize the sensations of stress, tension, and relaxation.

Breathing Better

There are all kinds of breathing techniques that can be used as relaxation tools. The examples explained below are just a few of the options available to you.

Whichever breathing form or technique you choose, your primary goal should be to bring regularity to your breathing in order to relax your body and calm your mind. Just like with your mindfulness practices, try to set aside some time each day to engage in a breathing exercise.

Simple Breathing Technique

This basic technique can be done while sitting, standing, or lying down. The only goal is to focus on regulating your breathing:

1. Inhale slowly through your nose, allowing your abdomen to expand and your chest to rise.
2. Purse your lips, and exhale slowly through your mouth, even making a soft whooshing sound as you breathe out.
3. Repeat this practice until you feel relaxed and calm.

Box Breathing

Box breathing is another simple breathing tool. It is also known as four square breathing, and it can be practiced easily in any position and at any time. It is a particularly useful strategy for very stressful moments of panic and anxiety.

To engage in this exercise, all you have to do is breathe in and out while holding the image of a square or box in your mind:

1. Inhale for a count of four, and imagine yourself moving along the top side of a box from left to right.
2. Hold your breath for four seconds, and picture yourself sliding down the right-hand side of your box.

3. Exhale for a count of four as you mentally move along the bottom side of your box.
4. Hold your breath again for four seconds, and see yourself moving up the left-hand side of the box.
5. Repeat these steps for as long as you like or need.

Alternate Nostril Breathing

Alternate nostril breathing is a slightly more complicated breathing exercise that requires practice and patience.

Start by finding a relaxed, seated position, and breathe in and out normally until you feel settled. Then take your dominant hand, and bend your middle and pointer fingers into your palm so that only your pinky, ring finger, and thumb are still extended.

Raise this hand to your nose, and use your thumb to close off your right nostril. You are then in the position to begin your breathing practice:

1. Inhale through the left nostril.
2. Close your left nostril with your ring finger so that both nostrils are now blocked.
3. Lift your thumb, and exhale through your right nostril.
4. Inhale through your right nostril.
5. Use your thumb to block your right nostril so that both nostrils are closed off again.

6. Lift your ring finger, and exhale through your left nostril.

This is one round of breathing: in through the left nostril, out through the right, in through the right, and out through the left.

Return to Step 1, and repeat this process for up to 10 rounds. Remember to go slowly and have patience while you get the hang of it.

Autogenic Relaxation

Autogenic means self-generated, and it refers to something that comes from within you.

The autogenic relaxation technique is one that involves using your own observations, awareness, and self-statements to induce a relaxed state. The idea is to repeat reassuring words to yourself as you observe—and thereby create—calmness within your body. Ultimately, you want to induce and then reinforce the body's natural relaxation response.

You will need about 20 minutes to complete this exercise, so set aside some time and find a quiet place where you will not be disturbed.

Start by getting yourself settled in a comfortable position, either sitting or lying down. Then practice this technique by bringing awareness to your body, and inserting calming self-statements:

1. First, bring awareness to your breathing. Breathe in and out slowly, find a regular rhythm, and notice the physical sensations of your chest rising and falling. Say to yourself, "I am breathing regularly, and I am completely calm."

2. Move on to observe the different parts of your body. Start with one of your arms, and say to yourself, “My right arm feels heavy, and I am completely calm.”

3. Repeat this process for your other arm and both your legs. You can also induce warmness when observing your different body parts by saying, for example, “My left leg feels warm, and I am completely calm.”

4. Finally, notice your own heartbeat by observing its rhythm and physical sensation. Breathe deeply, and say to yourself multiple times, “My heartbeat is regular and calm, so I am completely calm.”

Progressive Muscle Relaxation

Progressive muscle relaxation is similar to the paired muscle relaxation technique used in TIPP (see Chapter 3 on distress tolerance). Both of these relaxation techniques focus on using a relaxed physical state to induce a calm emotional state.

To practice progressive muscle relaxation, do as the name suggests: Focus progressively on one group of muscles at a time, alternately tensing and then relaxing them.

This exercise will also take around 20 minutes to complete, so make sure that you set aside enough uninterrupted time. Start by finding a quiet place where you can sit or lie down, and make sure to get comfortable before you begin:

1. Deliberately relax your entire body, and take a few deep, slow breaths.
2. Turn your attention to your toes, and deliberately lift all of them upwards—or point them all downwards—in order to tense both your feet.
3. Hold this tension for around 5 seconds.
4. Relax your position, and rest for 30 seconds.
5. Move on to your calves, and tense these muscles by pointing your toes or flexing your feet.
6. Hold this tension for 5 seconds, then let go and relax for 30 seconds.
7. Similarly, tense your thighs for 5 seconds, and then relax for 30 seconds.
8. Continue moving up your body progressively, tensing the remaining muscle groups: your buttocks, stomach muscles, hands, arms, shoulders, and facial muscles. Remember to hold this tension for 5 seconds, and to rest in between for 30 seconds.

The more you practice this technique, the more familiar you will become with the sensations of tension and relaxation. This will help you in everyday life to notice your own stress and anxiety, and it should be a sign to yourself to employ a relaxation strategy.

Visualization

Visualization is a relaxation technique that is similar to the distress tolerance tool of imagery (see Chapter 3). Both of these techniques involve using mental images and your own imagination to help you relax your mind and body.

Visualization can be done anywhere and at any time, but at the start of your practice, it is best to find a quiet place where you won't be disturbed:

1. Close your eyes, and sit quietly for a few moments. Focus on your breathing, and ground yourself in the present moment.

2. Once you are settled, begin your visual journey by thinking of a specific place, situation, person, or experience that brings you peace and comfort.

3. After you've chosen your fantasy, start to fill in the details to really immerse yourself. Mentally picture yourself in this place or experience, and imagine how calm and peaceful it would make you feel.

4. Engage fully by using all of your senses: Imagine what you would see, touch, taste, hear, and smell in your visualization. For example, if you are picturing a relaxing sunrise at the ocean, imagine the smell of the sea, the sound of the waves, the feel of the sand, the taste of the air, and the sight of the sun and sea.

5. Continue with your visualization until you feel that your body has physically relaxed and that your mind and emotions have calmed.

Relaxing Activities

In addition to these structured techniques, there are other simple and easy things that you can do in order to reduce your stress and anxiety.

For example, be more mindful of how you spend your free time, and try to engage in relaxing activities more regularly:

- Go for a massage or spa treatment every once in a while.
- Take a weekly yoga or tai chi class to incorporate movement and breathing in your daily life.
- Engage in art and creative expression through painting, drawing, or writing.
- Listen to music, or play an instrument.
- Read a book in the park.
- Try aromatherapy by lighting aroma candles and sticks, using essential body oils, or wearing aromatherapy accessories.
- Spend more time in nature.
- Practice simple hydrotherapy by taking a warm bath to relax after a long day.

CHAPTER 6: EMOTIONAL REGULATION

In addition to distress tolerance, mindfulness, and relaxation, learning how to regulate your emotions is a vital tool for dealing with the stress and anxiety of mental health challenges.

People struggling with their mental health often feel overwhelmed by the storm of their own emotions. They are confused by what they are feeling, and they are not always able to identify their emotions clearly. Moreover, their daily functioning is impacted because they regularly become too upset to think clearly, relax, sleep, study, work, or deal with people.

Emotional regulation tools are important skills that combat these struggles by helping people to understand and control their emotions. These techniques aim to build emotional resilience and stability, and to give people greater insight into their own feelings.

Trust That Feeling

In a biological sense, emotions have a practical and evolutionary purpose. They are meant to communicate information about our surroundings, and to guide us toward an appropriate action in response to an external trigger. For example, the emotion of fear lets us know that there is danger nearby, and it pushes us to run away, hide, or prepare to fight.

Because of this strong link between emotion and the urge to act, we need to be able to trust our emotional triggers. Are they pushing us to make the right choices, or have we learned inappropriate responses?

This is where self-destructive and harmful impulses become relevant again. Having a poorly regulated and overly sensitive emotional system can mean that we are always looking for immediate relief, and the quick fixes we choose to employ often do more harm than good (see Chapter 3 on the problem with temporary relief).

To counteract these problems, emotional regulation techniques aim to help us understand, control, and regulate our own emotions. These strategies are about being able to influence the nature of your emotions, as well as when you have them and how intensely you experience them.

After practicing these tools, you should be able to achieve the overall goals of the emotional regulation framework:

- You should be able to identify and label your emotions as you experience them.
- You will be able to reduce your vulnerability to emotion, and build your emotional resilience.
- You will be able to decrease your emotional suffering by limiting your experience of negative emotions.

To start you off, the first technique we will explore uses the rules of stop, take a step back, observe, and proceed (STOP) to help you to stay in control of yourself during an emotional experience.

STOP

The STOP tool is easy and simple to implement in moments when you are feeling confused by your own emotions, and don't know what to do about your feelings.

The aim of STOP is to decrease your susceptibility to emotional triggers, and to prevent you from acting impulsively without thinking. These steps will also help you to gain better clarity on your emotional state, and they will ensure that you move forward with emotional stability.

Stop

If you are feeling emotionally overwhelmed and out of control, the first thing to do is to stop.

This means that you physically stop moving. Remain frozen on the spot until you feel yourself calm down, and until the urge to act with impulse has passed.

Take a Step Back

The next principle of STOP is to take a step back from the situation in order to give yourself time and space to think clearly.

This can be done literally by physically moving away from the stressor, or figuratively by just thinking about something else for a moment.

The aim of this step is to bring yourself to a calmer emotional state, so you can even implement a distress tolerance, mindfulness, or relaxation strategy to assist you with this.

Observe

Once you have the time and space to do so, objectively assess what it is that you are feeling.

This means noticing your emotions, as well as the urges they are triggering, and trying to label these feelings clearly. To this end, you can implement the mindfulness tools you learned earlier, or you can see the next section for specific guidance on identifying and labeling emotions.

Proceed

The final step of STOP is to proceed mindfully by weighing up the information you have objectively observed. This means using this information to make a logical decision about your next step.

It can also help to ask yourself some key questions: What are my goals here?; what choice will help this situation?; and what will make this situation worse? Your overall aim should be to use your understanding of your emotions to make a rational decision about your future behavior. You will have to choose either to accept or reject the action being triggered by your feelings, and in making this choice, you want to prioritize constructive and healthy behavior.

Proceeding mindfully is also important for ensuring something called value engagement. When we act impulsively, we often go against our own core values, which can cause additional emotional distress and confusion. On the other hand, when we stop to think carefully about our emotions and behaviors, we are more likely to give ourselves the chance to act in line with our central beliefs and characteristics. This congruence is important for cultivating a stable sense of self, which is key for maintaining good mental health.

Identifying and Labeling

Learning to identify and label your own feelings is not only useful as part of the STOP skill, but it is also crucial for regulating your emotions in a more general sense. The goal of this technique is to teach you to notice your own feelings, and to put a name or label to those emotions in order to make them more manageable.

Over time, this tool will help you to become more aware and mindful of your own feelings. It will also give you a greater understanding of the different things you are likely to feel in different situations, which will make your emotional experiences a lot less frightening and confusing. The more familiar you become with your own feelings, the easier they will be to deal with and regulate.

Identifying and labeling emotions is a process of combining emotional, physical, and behavioral awareness in order to better understand and regulate yourself:

1. Start by paying attention to your emotions nonjudgmentally. As with mindfulness, simply note what you are feeling, and try not to critique or judge yourself for whatever emotion you are experiencing.

2. Notice the physical sensations and thoughts that are linked to your emotions: racing thoughts, rapid heartbeat, shakiness, a flushed face, and physical discomfort. This awareness will help you to identify your specific emotions more easily as you become more familiar with their effects on your body and mind.

3. Note any behavioral impulses that you are experiencing. Consider what your emotions might be trying to tell you about your environment, and determine the purpose of the emotion. Ask yourself what your emotions are pushing you to do, and why.

4. Give your emotions a name. Run through a list of possible options in your head, like anger, sadness, shame, loneliness, depression, and anxiety, and decide on which emotion you are feeling.

5. Write down that emotion to make it more concrete and real for you, and link this label to the other observations you made in Step 2 and Step 3.

6. Address your emotions with kindness. Validate your emotions by acknowledging what you are feeling, and provide yourself with comfort and positive self-talk if you are feeling particularly distressed.

7. Decide whether to listen to the emotion, or to let it go. Determine whether you can trust the action being encouraged by the emotion, and evaluate the next best step to take.

Opposite Action Skill

When deciding on your next step, you can use another emotional regulation tool called the opposite action skill.

This strategy provides a guide for how to behave when you want to reject the action being encouraged by your emotions. In doing so, this skill also teaches you how to limit negative feelings, change unwanted emotions, and replace harmful urges.

Reducing Negative Emotions

The theory behind this skill is that, if you want an emotion to become less distressing or to disappear entirely, you should do the opposite of the action it is pushing you toward.

For example, the feeling of shame will make you want to hide and isolate yourself. To reduce this negative feeling, do an opposite action like raising your head, making eye contact, or seeking out interpersonal contact. Similarly, depression will encourage you toward inactivity, so the opposite action is to be active in some way. In the same way, anger might push you to attack and act with aggression, so you can minimize this emotion by walking away or acting with gentleness.

Changing Unwanted Emotions

The opposite action skill is also useful for manipulating emotions when they do not fit in with the facts. You can use this tool to change unwanted emotional triggers in situations where they do not serve a reasonable purpose.

For example, you might experience fear right before you have to give a presentation at work. This fear may trigger the urge to run away, but you know that this would not be the appropriate response. In order to change this emotional experience and behavioral trigger, you can implement the opposite action skill, and deliberately act with confidence and calmness.

Replacing Harmful Urges

In the same way, the opposite action skill can help you to respond constructively to a negative emotion that is pushing you toward self-destructive behavior.

For example, if you are feeling a painful emotion that is prompting you to engage in harmful actions, deliberately do an opposite and productive activity instead. This can be running an errand, cleaning your room, or going for a walk—anything healthy to replace the negative urges. Over time, with consistency and practice, the harmful impulses will dissipate, and they will be replaced by urges toward productive activity.

Cope Ahead

A final tool for emotional regulation is the cope ahead skill. This technique works to reduce your vulnerability to emotional distress by helping you to prepare adequately in advance for stressful situations. It is a particularly useful strategy to employ when you are feeling overwhelmed by fear, worry, and anxiety in relation to future events.

There are two specific benefits to planning ahead. Firstly, you will have more confidence when it comes to actually dealing with the situation, so you will be able to cope better with the task itself. Secondly, you will feel more in control of your emotions leading up to the task, so you will experience less emotional distress overall.

The idea is to pinpoint exactly which situation or task is causing you to feel overwhelmed, and to manage this emotional whirlwind by working through the problem in advance:

1. Describe the problem fully by sticking to the facts and being specific. Remember to reserve judgment, and to use objective words and labels for the actions and emotions involved.

2. Decide on how you are going to deal with the situation by choosing an appropriate problem-solving skill or coping mechanism given the nature of the issue.

3. Rehearse the process of coping by imaging exactly how you are going to solve the problem. Work through the steps involved, and consider how you will deal with any obstacles that might arise. Try to be as vivid as possible in your imaginings, and remember to insert yourself directly into the fantasy.

4. Plan for success by rehearsing a positive outcome. You can do this by imagining how well you will cope with the situation, even if the worst-case scenario unfolds.

CHAPTER 7: ADDRESSING NEGATIVE THOUGHTS

As we saw in Chapter 6, emotional regulation is about being able to influence your emotions in order to gain more control and feel less overwhelmed. Similarly, there are several tools that you can use to address your own thoughts.

Many people who suffer from mental health conditions struggle with automatic negative thoughts and cognitive distortions, which impact how they see themselves and the world around them. But the good news is that it is never too late to change how you think.

The techniques of this chapter go to the heart of CBT and its foundational theory that our beliefs impact our emotions, which then shape our actions. If we can understand and influence our thought patterns, then we can then better regulate our emotions and control our behavior.

Thoughts and Beliefs

Much of the emotional distress we feel originates in the way that we think about ourselves and our lives. We can get so caught up in how we are feeling and what we are doing that we do not notice the extensive impact of our own thoughts and beliefs. Moreover, many of us struggle with problematic thinking patterns without ever understanding where these negative beliefs and thoughts come from.

Automatic Negative Thoughts

Automatic negative thoughts are one example of how disordered thinking can lead to emotional and behavioral distress. These are the negative thoughts that pop into your head right after something has happened, making you feel upset and overwhelmed.

While they are usually triggered by an external stimulus, automatic negative thoughts are actually related to emotions and experiences that we have internalized throughout our lives. They are a type of negative self-talk that is driven by the core beliefs that we hold about ourselves and the world around us.

Not only can these thoughts be emotionally distressing, but they can also push us toward problematic and self-destructive behaviors. Most commonly, we see a pattern of negative and self-fulfilling behavior as a result.

For example, imagine you are given a new assignment at work, but you find yourself struggling with an automatic negative thought like, *I always fail, and I am not good at my job*. This can lead you to feel insecure, depressed, and worthless, and as a result of these emotions, you do not try very hard to do the task well. The result may then be that you do in fact fail. This reinforces the initial belief you had even though it was your unique actions in this case that led to the failure and not the belief itself.

Cognitive Distortions

Cognitive distortions are another example of disordered thinking. These are inherent thinking patterns that are not based in reality or fact, but are internal biases and filters. Cognitive distortions cause people to view the world incorrectly, and to develop faulty beliefs about themselves and others.

There are several common categories of cognitive distortions, and becoming familiar with these disordered patterns can help you to recognize your own biased thinking:

- Catastrophizing is the habit of jumping to the conclusions without sufficient evidence. For example, thinking something like, *My son missed his curfew, so he must have been in a car accident.*

- Mind reading is assuming that you know what people are thinking, and that they are always thinking negatively about you. For example, *My coworker is never happy to work with me because she thinks I'm incompetent.*

- Polarized thinking is seeing things strictly as black or white, and thinking in all-or-nothing terms. For example, *I am a bad person because I made that mistake.*

- Overgeneralization is assuming the same conclusion for every situation. For example, *I failed the last test, so I will fail this one too.*

- Emotional reasoning is believing that emotions are facts, and that how you feel accurately reflects reality. For example, *I feel like a bad daughter, which means I am a bad daughter.*

- Personalization is thinking that everything is about you, affects you, or is your fault. For example, *We lost that game because I didn't play well.*

- Labeling is the tendency to classify and reduce everything to a single label or category. For example, *I didn't get that job because I am a failure.*

- Mental filtering means focusing only on the negative and ignoring the positives in every situation. For example, *I had fun at the party, but the host didn't greet me so I really should have stayed home.*

- Discounting the positives is about overlooking, dismissing, or explaining away the positives. For example, *I only did well because I got lucky.*

- "Should" statements indicate a belief that everything ought to happen in a particular way. For example, *I am 30 years old, so I should be married with children by now.*

As with automatic negative thoughts, it is important to learn about your own cognitive distortions as this can make them easier to address and reverse.

Fact-Checking

The first actionable technique for addressing thoughts and beliefs is fact-checking. This is a quick and easy tool that can be used on the spot. The aim is to confront faulty thoughts and beliefs right as they pop into your head, and before they can begin to cause you emotional distress.

Specifically, fact-checking is about being able to identify thoughts and beliefs that are masquerading in your head as facts. The idea is to learn that not all thoughts are objective truths, and that these thoughts do not have to hold such power over you. You do not have to believe them or let them influence your emotional state and behavior.

The practice of fact-checking is very simple:

1. Identify the thought that is affecting you.

2. Decide if this thought is a fact or an opinion.

And that's it. You don't necessarily have to do anything about the decision that you make in Step 2. The effectiveness of this tool is in how it helps you to gain more power over your own perception.

For example, imagine fact-checking the thought, *I missed that deadline at work because I am lazy and bad at my job*. The first part of this thought is an objective fact, but the second part is simply an opinion you hold about yourself. There may be a range of factors that explain why you missed the deadline, and by separating fact from opinion, you can avoid making a moral judgment about yourself. In other words, you don't have to let one event affect your entire sense of self-worth and capability.

Cognitive Restructuring

Cognitive restructuring is a more in-depth version of fact-checking. It can be used for more complicated situations where you aren't able to distinguish easily between facts and opinions.

Start by clearly identifying the specific thought that you suspect might be automatically negative or distorted. Then, begin to fact-check this thought by listing the facts that support it, as well as the facts that contradict it. Ask yourself what leads you to believe this thought might accurately reflect reality, and what makes you doubt that this thought is true.

Once you've finished with these pros and cons, you should have a more definitive idea about the nature of your thinking. You can then challenge yourself further by answering several questions about your thought patterns:

- Is the situation black and white, or is it made up of shades of gray?
- Are you making unjustified assumptions or misinterpreting the evidence?
- How might other people interpret the situation?
- Are you being biased by only including the evidence that supports your view?

- Are you maintaining your thoughts and beliefs simply out of habit?
- How did this thought come to you originally: Was it inspired by a situation or person, and is that originating factor reliable?
- How likely is the scenario that your thought brings up, and is it the worst-case scenario?

Having thoroughly investigated and challenged your thoughts with the above techniques, you can now move on to recording, reframing, and countering these patterns using the tools below.

Dysfunctional Thought Record

A dysfunctional thought record is a structured technique for evaluating your negative thoughts. The aim of creating this kind of record is to bring more awareness to these thoughts, and to help give you a better understanding of when, why, and how these thoughts might occur. It is a self-monitoring technique that encourages you to delve more deeply into your own thinking patterns and to actively search for more constructive alternatives.

Start by grabbing a piece of paper, taking out your journal, or pulling up a note-taking application on your phone or computer. Create a table with seven columns in order to investigate a specific thought:

1. In your first column, write down the date and time that your thought occurred.
2. In the second column, describe the facts of the situation or event during which you had this thought.

3. Use the third column to describe the exact nature of the thought.
4. Focus on emotions in your fourth column, and write down all of the emotions elicited by the thought, as well as an intensity scale indicating your experience of each emotion.
5. In your fifth column, determine which of the above cognitive distortions is behind your thought.
6. In the sixth column, brainstorm an alternative positive thought or more constructive way of viewing the situation.
7. Use your seventh and final column to explore the outcome of the exercise by summarizing how you feel and think in the aftermath.

You can create as many rows as there are thoughts that you want to investigate, and you can easily add them to your table as you practice this tool. **A Worked Example:**

Date	**Event**	**Thought**	**Emotion**	**Distortion**	**Alternative**	**Outcome**
May 10, 10 a.m.	I saw my friend, Sarah, today and greeted her, but she ignored me.	*Sarah doesn't like me.* *She must think I'm boring.* *She doesn't want to be my friend anymore.*	Sadness (90%) Anxiety (80%) Anger (30%) Insecurity (100%)	Mind reading	*Sarah might not have even seen me.* *Perhaps she was busy and distracted.* *I am a good friend, and worthy of friendship.*	I feel much less anxious and insecure after thinking more rationally. I feel happier after reminding myself that I am a good friend.

Cognitive Reframing

Coming up with alternative thoughts and solutions for the sixth column of your dysfunctional thought record can be difficult, but this cognitive reframing is one of the most important steps for changing your own thinking.

Cognitive reframing is about consciously working to reframe your own thoughts and perceptions. The goal of this technique is to notice when you are stuck in a cycle of negative thinking, and to retrain your thoughts by finding something more positive and productive to focus on. The more consistently you practice this tool, the easier and more automatic it will become. Over time, you will be able to reinforce for yourself that there are always different ways to view every situation.

Positive Thought Replacement

One way to use cognitive reframing is through positive thought replacement.

For example, let's say that you walk into a room and immediately think, *I hate the color of these walls.* You can practice thought replacement by noticing this negativity and then consciously trying to find something more positive to focus on. In this example, this would mean choosing something about the room that you do like, and replacing your initial negativity with your new thought such as, *This room gets really great light.*

Counteractive Self-Statements

Cognitive reframing can also involve using counteractive self-statements to change how you think about yourself.

For example, perhaps you experience a romantic breakup, and your first thought in response to this undesirable event is something like, *I am unlovable, and I will never find someone to be happy with*. In this situation, you can counter this negativity, and actively build yourself up, through a positive self-statement such as, *I have value and worth, and I will be happy one day*.

You can also use this cognitive reframing tool for everyday, seemingly mundane incidents. For example, when we make little mistakes like forgetting to make a doctor's appointment, we often automatically talk down to ourselves by thinking, *Oh, I'm such an idiot*. This may seem insignificant and harmless, but we have learned in this chapter that our thoughts can impact our emotions and beliefs in all kinds of insidious ways. As such, it is important to notice this kind of negativity, and to counter it by thinking a positive self-statement like, *I'm only human, and we all make mistakes*.

CHAPTER 8: JOURNALING

The previous chapter suggested several techniques that are best practiced as written down exercises, so this is a good place to explore journaling as a tool for mental health.

As this chapter will show, journaling is an effective way to reflect on yourself and your past experiences, as well as to monitor your daily functioning. You can also use journaling to conduct different thought experiments that will help you to address your anxieties about the future.

Self-Reflection

Journaling is a practical means of expression, and an easy way to get your thoughts and feelings out of your own head. It can be particularly helpful for reflecting on how different experiences make you feel, and for exploring why you feel and act the way that you do. Journaling can allow you to gain a broader perspective on your experiences and feelings, and ultimately, the more concretely and frequently you deal with these parts of yourself, the less overwhelming they will become.

When deciding how best to use your journal, keep in mind that it is a very personal tool, so it can be as informal as you like. You can choose how often you write in it, and what you write about.

Ultimately, the goals of journaling are simple: to relieve your emotional burden, notice common thoughts patterns, practice describing your emotions, and brainstorm different coping mechanisms.

Free Form

If you enjoy writing, and you prefer to express yourself in an unrestrained way, then you can use your journal as a personal diary.

You can write in free form about different events and situations, and explore how these things make you feel. You can record your own stream of consciousness, and elaborate on anything and everything that might come to your mind.

If you use this method, it is a good idea to remember to read back your words every so often so that you are really reflecting on the situation and your patterns of thought, emotion, and behavior. The purpose of journaling for mental health is not only to put words to your struggles, but also to learn more about yourself.

Writing Prompts

If you find yourself with writer's block, or if you would prefer more guidance when investigating your inner consciousness, you can use specific prompting questions to kick-start your journaling:

- What happened today? Was there a triggering or stressful event?
- What are you thinking about today? What thoughts did you have in response to specific events?

- What are you feeling? How intense is your experience of these emotions? Why might you be feeling this way?
- What has your behavior been like? What have you done today, and why?

ABC Model

If writing in the free form is not for you, there are many structured ways of journaling as well. For example, you can fill your journal with dysfunctional thought records, emotion labeling exercises, or sets of cognitive restructuring questions. There is also another structured journaling technique available to you called the ABC model.

The ABC model is a more formal exercise that aims to give you a better understanding of how your beliefs affect your emotions and behaviors. Specifically, it is based on the belief that all life experiences are made up of three components: activating events, beliefs, and consequences. In other words, something happens to you (activating event), you think a certain way about what happened (beliefs), and then you feel or act in a specific way as a result (consequences).

The usefulness of this technique is in how it encourages us to identify all three of these aspects: Specifically, it pushes you not to overlook how beliefs affect what kind of consequences the activating events will have. Your goal should be to find that essential correlation between beliefs and consequences so that you can develop more constructive ways of thinking.

To carry out this exercise, you first need to set out a table in your journal with three columns for the activating event, the belief, and the consequences. While your table will be in the order of ABC reading left to right, the practical steps of this model jump around a bit:

1. Start with identifying the consequences by choosing which behavior or emotion you want to address. Write down these actions or feelings in your table's third column.

2. Look at the activating event, and describe the situation in which you experienced the above consequences. Write these details down in your first column.

3. Find the belief involved in this life experience by determining why you felt or acted the way you did. Ask yourself what the activating event meant to you, and elaborate on what you were thinking at the time. Write these beliefs down in the middle column of your table.

4. Reflect on the connection by reading your table in the order of ABC. This should help you to see how your beliefs about the activating event shaped your consequences in a particular way.

5. Challenge your beliefs if they are causing an undesirable consequence. You can actively address any negative and distorted thoughts using the techniques in Chapter 7.

A Worked Example

To see how different thoughts can affect the consequences of an event, consider the two examples in the table below. Here, you can see how the same activating event leads to different consequences depending on the thinking that took place in between.

Activating Event	Beliefs	Consequences
I hear children playing in the street outside my house.	I think about my own childhood spent playing with my siblings.	I feel happy and nostalgic, and I call my sister to see how she is.
I hear children playing in the street outside my house.	I think that I need to work and that the children are being disruptive and loud.	I feel irritable and angry, and I go outside to yell at the children.

Self-Monitoring

You can also use your journal as a self-monitoring tool to track your moods, activities, and habits.

Activity Tracking

Your journal is not only a great place to investigate your thoughts and feelings, but it is also somewhere for you to explore your habits and behaviors in more detail.

You can use your journal to think more carefully about the activities taking up your time. You can consider whether these things are adding to or taking away from your mental health. For example, are you devoting enough time to your interpersonal relationships? Do you have enough time to rest and relax? Are you making time for exercise and movement? Your journal is also where you can outline any goals that you have with respect to these aspects of your life.

Another way to maximize your own activity tracking is to create weekly to-do lists and schedules for yourself. This will make your self-monitoring relatively easy, and it will also help you to feel more organized and motivated for your daily tasks.

Chapter 9 will explore activity scheduling, behavior activation, and goal setting in more detail, but for now, keep in mind that your mental health journal is a great place to deal with these concepts.

Mood Tracking

Similarly, it is a good idea to track your mood alongside your activities and tasks. This is so that you can more clearly identify how different things make you feel. You can then focus on what makes you feel good, and you can also reduce your engagement in activities that have a negative effect on your mood.

You can track your mood in whatever way makes the most sense to you, but one option is to write down the emotions that you experienced during an activity. You can then add a numerical rating to indicate to yourself how intense that emotional experience was for you. For example, you can rate each emotion on a scale of one to five, with one representing a mild experience and five being a severe emotion.

If you are more visually minded, you can come up with symbols to represent your moods, or you can draw little smiley face pictures alongside your activities to indicate to yourself how you felt about them.

Overall, your goal is to be able to identify any stressors in your life. This will ensure that you are able to monitor your energy levels and emotional capacity effectively. You can then make adjustments to your schedule accordingly.

Thought Experiments

Journaling can also be used to work through future events that cause anxiety and worry. Just the act of writing down your concerns can provide comfort and security. By using words to verbalize your fears, you can turn them into something tangible and manageable.

There are also structured thought experiments that can guide you through ways of coping with these emotions.

Play the Script

Playing the script to the end is one such tool that aims to help you confront your fears and anxieties about a specific scenario.

The goal of this technique is to imagine the outcome of the worst-case scenario, and then to recognize that, even if the worst does happen, the situation will still be manageable.

Similar to the cope ahead skill, this thought experiment will give you a sense of confidence and capability about the situation. It helps you to develop a plan of action, which allows you to de-escalate the situation for yourself.

To play the script to the end, simply write down and explore the answers to these questions in your journal:

1. What am I worried about?
2. How likely is it that this thing happens?
3. If it does, what's the worst that could then happen?
4. If the worst does happen, what will I do?

CHAPTER 9: MOTIVATION AND PURPOSE

Chapter 8 highlighted how useful it can be to monitor your own activity and mood. Living more consciously in this way is important for avoiding behaviors that negatively affect your mood, and for working toward the end goal of good mental health. Overall, it is essential to figure out how to live a life of purpose and meaning that you can feel good about.

The foundational ingredient for living deliberately and with purpose is having the motivation to do so. As such, this chapter outlines several tools that are designed to improve your motivation. These are practical techniques for determining what behaviors and activities are fulfilling and important to you, and for encouraging and motivating yourself to engage in them.

Activity Scheduling

The previous chapter mentioned how to-do lists and activity monitoring can help you to feel more organized and motivated on a daily basis. This thinking is underpinned by the CBT theory surrounding activity scheduling. The idea behind this technique is that the simple act of scheduling, planning, and organizing is enough to boost a person's mood.

Activity scheduling is most commonly used to help people who are struggling with depression, isolation, and inertia, and it is designed to improve motivation, enthusiasm, and drive. This is because having specific things to look forward to helps you to sustain a good outlook about the future.

Moreover, getting yourself to engage in these planned activities sparks off a positive cycle of improved mood, increased motivation, and more activity. The sense of reward you feel from following through on your plans encourages you to make more plans for the future.

Scheduling in Practice

In practice, activity scheduling means actively planning activities that you can engage in on a daily and weekly basis.

To kick off this exercise, start by deciding where you will do your scheduling. You can use your journal from Chapter 8 to set out a calendar, or you can use the digital calendar on your phone or computer. You can also buy a weekly planner, which you can stick up on a wall in your room, or you can invest in a dated diary, which you can keep with you in your bag. The idea is to use whatever is easiest for you, and to do your scheduling in whichever way you prefer.

Having decided on the means, remember to set aside some time at the beginning of each week during which you can do your planning. Take a look at your calendar, and start by filling in your unavoidable obligations: when you have to go to work or when your time is taken up by other responsibilities.

You should now have a much clearer idea of your free time and of how much extra time you have for other activities each week. It is this time that you will target for activity scheduling, and the goal is simply to write down the activities that you plan to engage in.

How to Decide What to Do

When deciding on your activities, remember to start by keeping it simple. It wouldn't be feasible to be continuously scheduling fancy dinner parties, extensive outings, and big family gatherings. Rather, redefine what activity means for you, and keep in mind that you can—and should—include a lot of small and easy behaviors: calling a friend, watching a movie at home, sitting quietly in the garden, or having a cup of tea in the afternoon.

Another important thing to remember when choosing your activities is that you should focus on what is fun and pleasant. The basis of activity scheduling theory is that engaging in tasks that are pleasant is what helps to boost your mood, motivation, and enthusiasm. So, doing the laundry or cleaning the kitchen are not necessarily well-chosen activities—unless, of course, these are things that you personally enjoy. Remember that fun is subjective, and that all you need for activity scheduling is something that you find to be pleasant.

As such, the final guiding rule for activity scheduling is to draw from activities that you already engage in. Take a look at the different areas of your life, and consider your existing hobbies and interests: running, yoga, volunteering, reading, writing, golf, chess, art, watching films, or gardening. Whatever they might be, use these existing hobbies to fill up your activity schedule.

Behavior Activation

Another way to determine which activities are best to focus on in activity scheduling is to use a closely related concept called behavior activation.

This is a technique whereby you use your own behavior to influence your emotions. The goal of behavior activation is to engage deliberately in positive behaviors in order to activate a positive emotional state.

It is important to keep in mind that the opposite is also true, and that engaging in unhealthy and negative behaviors will negatively affect your mood and thinking.

Categorizing Behavior

In order to correctly activate positive emotions, you will first need to know which activities and tasks are positive behaviors for you, as well as which are negative. Start by taking a look at your activity schedule, and creating a log of your behaviors to categorize them as either positive or negative.

Positive behaviors will be the things that are healthy and fulfilling, and that make you feel good. These can be conventionally healthy activities, like exercise and spending time with loved ones, or they can be unique and personal hobbies. Moreover, positive behaviors can also include small and simple tasks like self-care activities and personal hygiene habits.

On the other hand, negative behaviors are those that make you feel bad, and that cause unpleasant feelings like worthlessness, anxiety, insecurity, and depression. These can be explicitly harmful behaviors, such as excessive drinking and drug use, or they can be less obvious and more personal. For example, if you know that spending too much time watching TV is something that lowers your mood and motivation, then this will be a negative behavior for you as an individual.

Helping Yourself

Once you have finished categorizing your activities and tasks, you will have a better idea of which behaviors to engage in more regularly than others. In order to activate positive emotions, remember to center your activity scheduling on your personal positive behaviors.

It is also a good idea to have a few chosen positive behaviors that you know you can rely on to make yourself feel better. For example, if you are having a bad week, and want to boost your mood and motivation, keep a list of little tasks that you can use to activate this positivity. These can be simple things like making the bed each day or cooking yourself a proper meal for dinner. You can view these behaviors as stopgap measures that prevent your mood from spiraling downward, and to motivate you back to a positive path.

Similarly, you can use behavior activation to get yourself out of a crisis state. If you notice that you are increasing your engagement in negative behaviors, this can be an indication that you are more distressed than you may realize. Take this as a sign to make a change, and deliberately start to replace your negative behaviors with more positive activities. You can then monitor your progress to track how your mood and motivation slowly improve.

Goal Setting

Self-initiation is an important part of both activity scheduling and behavior activation. The positive consequences of these techniques—improved mood and motivation—do not appear when you are being prompted or forced by someone else to engage in an activity or behavior. As such, what is really important about these strategies is that they are driven by your own decision-making.

One way to ensure that you are self-initiating and making your own choices is to set goals in relation to your behavior. Goal setting can also help you to identify what you really want, as well as how to get it. Moreover, the ability to set and achieve goals is a well-known strategy for lessening depression and boosting mood and motivation.

In practice, goal setting is a simple and easy technique:

1. Start by clearly identifying the goal, and determining the end result that you want to achieve.

2. Then take stock of the present situation in order to find your starting point. This means figuring out where things currently stand so that you know how far you need to go to achieve your goal.

3. Plan the steps to achieve your goal using small and accomplishable stages, and consider any obstacles that may arise.

4. Get started on the first step toward achieving your goal.

It is also important to remember to troubleshoot this process if you are not able to meet your goals. Rather than giving up or changing your goal entirely, take a closer look at why you might not have been able to perform as you planned. For example, perhaps you have not defined your goal clearly enough, or the steps of your plan are not small enough.

The best way to succeed in goal setting is to make sure that your goals are specific, measurable, achievable, relevant, and timely (SMART).

Specific

The first rule of SMART goal setting is that your goals need to be specific. This means that you should avoid vagueness, and be as clear as possible when making your goals.

For example, instead of making the goal of just wanting to exercise more, you can be much more specific by aiming to walk around the block every second day for a month.

Measurable

The SMART tool also dictates that your goal needs to be measurable. This is because you need to be able to track your progress.

For the example above, you would be able to track how many days of the month you walked, as well as how far around the block you were able to get.

Achievable

The "A" in SMART stands for achievable, which means that your goal needs to be possible given your present situation. Here, it is helpful to go back to Step 2 of the goal setting process in order to evaluate your starting point. Ultimately, you need to set a goal that is attainable by considering all current factors that might be relevant, such as your physical health, mental state, and amount of free time.

For example, your exercise goal can't be to run a marathon within the month if you have only just started out with your walking.

Relevant

Your goals also need to be relevant to the issue, problem, or area of your life that you are trying to address or improve.

For example, walking around the block is a good goal if you want to improve your physical health, but not if you want to meet other people who also exercise. To achieve that goal, you would be best served by aiming to join a gym or the local running group.

Timely

Finally, SMART encourages you to make a goal that fits into the timing of your life. In other words, it should be an appropriate time for you to be making whatever goal you have decided on.

For example, your walking goal would not be timely if you are still busy recovering from a long illness.

Finding Purpose

The final strategy for this chapter is about maximizing the potential of everything we have already discussed.

The goal of finding purpose and meaning in your life should guide your activity scheduling, behavior activation, and goal setting. This is because knowing what is important to you can help you to match up your behavior and your values. This value engagement is what will ensure that you can live a life that you feel good about.

Value Engagement

As such, the first step to finding purpose and meaning in your life is to figure out what your core values and beliefs are.

This means exploring what is most important to you, what you enjoy, and what makes you happy. It involves deciding what you want to live for, and figuring out what will make your life worth living.

It is important to take a lot of time to reflect on these aspects and characteristics about yourself. You can also review your work in this chapter in order to pinpoint patterns and commonalities in your enjoyable activities, positive behaviors, and goals.

Ultimately, you want to come up with a list of potential values that give your life purpose: creativity, work, productivity, quality time with others, relationships, romance, caregiving, animals, nature, sacrifice, responsibility, family, religion, culture, art, or health. Once you have decided on what is most important to you, you can reinforce your discoveries by linking each value to your activities and behavior.

You can do this visually by making up a table in your journal or calendar in order to illustrate your value engagement. Start by writing down a value on one side of the page, and then connect it with activities on the other side (see the example below). Remember to keep this information nearby so that, going forward, you can make sure that your purpose and meaning align well with how you spend your time.

Value	**Activity**
Family	Go for coffee with my sister. Attend family lunch on Sundays. Call my parents at least once a week.
Health	Go for a run at least three times a week. Attend yoga class twice a week. Cook a proper dinner each night.
Creativity	Write one short story a month. Visit the local art museum. Attend the weekly poetry reading at the local library.

CHAPTER 10: PROBLEM-SOLVING

Another set of skills that will help you to maximize the benefit of the behavioral tools and techniques of Chapter 9 is being able to solve problems. In fact, problem-solving is useful for dealing with obstacles that may arise during the course of engaging with any of the strategies outlined in this book.

Ultimately, problem-solving is an essential life skill because it is normal to be confronted with obstacles in our everyday lives. Learning how to cope effectively with these problems and challenges is vital for ensuring emotional well-being and good mental health.

Finding Solutions

Worry is the natural response to being confronted with a problem, and since life is filled with ups and downs, it is normal to experience this stress regularly. However, it is when we don't have the right set of skills to deal with our anxiety effectively, and to move on with our lives, that we can turn everyday problems into overwhelming and insurmountable obstacles.

As such, finding and applying effective problem–solving techniques is essential for good mental health. The goal of these techniques is to make your problem manageable, and to give you a sense of capability and confidence. This will not only reduce your anxiety and panic about facing your problems, but it will give you the clarity of mind and emotional stability to actually solve those problems.

Brainstorming

You will likely be familiar with the traditional problem-solving technique of brainstorming. This technique involves several steps that can be easily applied to whatever problem you facing:

1. Start by defining the problem clearly. This means setting aside time to investigate exactly what it is that is worrying you. Remember to focus on the facts, and to be specific when describing the situation to yourself.

2. Brainstorm any and all solutions to the problem. It is crucial to be entirely nonjudgmental, and not to reject any ideas for being too silly or outlandish: You don't know yet which ideas might have potential.

3. Weigh the advantages and disadvantages of each of your solutions from Step 2. This is where you rationally decide which ideas have merit given the circumstances.

4. Choose the most viable solution based on your logical investigation.

5. Make a plan to implement your chosen solution. This means outlining as many steps as necessary to make your solution actionable and achievable.

6. Put your solution into practice by starting with your planned first step.
7. Evaluate if your solution has worked by setting aside time to reflect on the problem-solving process. If you find that your solution was not effective, then return to Step 4 and make a different choice.

Prioritizing

In addition to practicing the technique above, another helpful way to deal with problems is to prioritize in different ways.

If you are feeling overwhelmed by several problems that span across multiple areas of your life, it can be difficult to know where to start. As such, prioritizing is useful for addressing this confusion and helplessness.

Values First

One way to make a situation like this more manageable is to prioritize according to your core values. This means focusing on your problems in the order of how important they are to you.

Start by taking a look at your value engagement table from Chapter 9 to remind yourself of your most important beliefs. Then move on to tackle the problems in the most important areas of your life. For example, if family is a very important value for you, then focus on your relationship and interpersonal problems first. If your career is less important, then put your occupational problems lower on your list of priorities.

Worry Time

Another important way to prioritize is with your time. It is vital to realize and remember that not all of your problems will be solved right away. In fact, most of your problems will take time to resolve, so it is not ideal to spend all of your time worrying about them. Instead, you can practice dividing up your time and compartmentalizing.

One way of doing this is by deliberately setting aside time for worrying during stressful periods. For example, allow yourself 15 minutes of worry time each day during which you can fixate and focus on your problems. You can spend this time writing down your problems and worries for the day, getting them out of your head, and confronting them more concretely. You can use the brainstorming technique to think up solutions, or you can simply sit and ruminate on the situation.

Crucially, once your official worry time is up, you can then move on with your day. The usefulness of worry time is that it helps you not to spend the whole day dwelling on your problems. The goal of this strategy is to get you to switch off from your worries when you are not actively solving problems.

If a problem does arise, or an anxious thought pops into your head, you should try to consciously set it aside for your worry time. For example, address this thought immediately with a counterstatement like, "I will worry about that later."

The foundation of your worry-free time should be about staying in the present, so mindfulness is a particularly helpful strategy for ignoring your nagging worries (see Chapter 4 for a reminder on how to live in the moment).

Ramping Up Relaxation

Prioritizing relaxation during stressful periods is another effective way to aid your problem-solving skills.

When you are faced with many obstacles and challenges it is important to increase your engagement in relaxation strategies (see Chapter 5 for ideas and guidance). This is because learning to relax will help to clear your mind, reduce the physical stress on your body, and regulate your emotions—all of which is vital for being able to see and solve a problem rationally.

Ignoring Hypothetical Problems

This final word on problem-solving is about the problems that you cannot solve. It is important to be able to recognize that some things are out of your control, and that those kinds of problems do not actually have a solution.

These hypothetical problems are usually easily identifiable as worries and anxieties that start with the phrase *what if*. For example, what if my partner breaks up with me? What if my parents get sick? What if I lose my job?

While these might be anxieties that cause you a lot of distress, and over which you frequently obsess, it is crucial to realize that they are not problems that you can solve. These are worries that are likely based in past experiences, as well as distorted thoughts and beliefs.

They are simply masquerading as problems, but in doing so, they put pressure on you to solve the unsolvable.

Practical Action

As such, it is vital that you learn to identify these hypothetical problems for what they are. One way to do this is by asking yourself if there is something practical that you can do to address the issue. If not, it is likely not a solvable problem, and trying to resolve it with problem-solving techniques will only lead to helplessness and frustration.

Instead, for these worries, try to find a more appropriate coping mechanism. Think about the other tools and techniques you have learned in this book, and employ a strategy that is more likely to be successful given the situation: radical acceptance, positive thought replacement, or playing the script to the end.

CHAPTER 11: SELF-ESTEEM

In recent chapters, we have worked on monitoring and activating behavior, finding motivation and purpose for these activities, and developing problem-solving skills to deal with any obstacles that might arise. This chapter aims to bring all of these tools together by addressing a final related concept: self-esteem.

Self-esteem is important for building a sense of capability and confidence. This goes hand in hand with boosting your mood and strengthening your motivation, purpose, and drive for life. As this chapter will explain, some of the best strategies for improving your self-esteem include building mastery by learning new skills and practicing positivity.

Why Is Self-Esteem Important?

Self-esteem is about how worthwhile you feel, and what kind of opinion you hold about yourself. It influences the confidence you have in your abilities, and it determines how much you respect yourself as a person.

Prioritizing your own self-esteem allows you to value yourself more consistently throughout life's many challenges. Having good self-esteem means that you can have a good relationship with yourself no matter the problems you may face. As such, self-esteem is important for your emotional resilience, and it is a crucial aid for the other strategies discussed in this book.

Not only is having good self-esteem incredibly beneficial for your mental health, but having poor self-esteem can be actively detrimental. It is exhausting and emotionally damaging to believe that you are not valuable, and poor self-esteem creates a negative mindset of worthlessness, depression, and insecurity. It can stop you from enjoying your life, and it prevents you from achieving your goals.

Moreover, people with a lack of self-esteem often get caught up in negative and self-fulling cycles. They live so continuously in the mindset that they don't deserve good things, or they can't do certain things, that they begin to believe this about themselves. As a result, they tend not to try their best—or at all—and they can even begin to self-sabotage, which only reinforces their lack of belief in themselves.

Building Mastery

Building mastery is an essential practical tool for boosting confidence and self-esteem. This technique is about learning to accomplish things for yourself in order to prove to yourself that you are strong, independent, and capable. The aim of the building mastery tool is to reduce feelings of helplessness and to increase your sense of control.

When you feel competent and confident, you can tackle your life and its problems with more ease and less emotional turbulence. The idea is that, if you regularly engage in your life with a sense of mastery, you can shift your mindset toward a more positive and confident outlook.

You will be able to reflect on your life and see yourself succeeding in your tasks and behaviors. You will start to think that you are capable and worthy, and over time, your self-esteem grows as you continue to gather evidence about your own competence.

Mastery in Practice

The first way to build mastery in practice is by doing something that you have done before, or that you already enjoy doing. Have another look at Chapter 9 to see how to use the tools of activity scheduling, behavior activation, and goal setting toward this end.

Having revised the best way to engage in your daily tasks and fun activities, channel this knowledge toward the build mastery tool by remembering a few key tips when practicing this technique:

- Do at least one thing a day that will build your own confidence in yourself. This can be something small and simple like doing the laundry.
- Plan to succeed by starting off with activities and tasks that you know are possible for you to do. Remember to make your goals realistic and achievable.
- Practice and repeat your chosen tasks until you feel a sense of capability and competency about these activities.
- Remember to persevere when things do not go as planned. Building mastery is about consistency and resilience, and the goal is to collect a wealth of evidence to prove to yourself that you are competent.

Openness to Experience

While practicing what you can already do is undoubtedly useful, building mastery is even more effectively done by trying new things, and by being open to new experiences.

Doing new things can exponentially increase your self-esteem and sense of capability. Only doing things that are easily accomplishable will not add to your competency forever, so remembering to challenge yourself is vitally important.

Engaging in new experiences is also a great way to improve your confidence, and to get yourself out of reinforcing cycles of isolation and inertia. It can open you up to new connections with others, and highlight new areas of purpose and meaning in your life.

The first step to partaking in new experiences is to make sure that you have the right mindset. This means maintaining an openness and eagerness in your activities and relationships, and being ready to accept any invitations and opportunities that may come your way.

Learning New Skills

Learning new skills is another approach to building mastery by doing new things. For this strategy, remember to keep it simple to start.

Learning new things does not have to be dramatic or scary, and you don't need to have any kind of qualification or experience. Simply focus on what you are interested in, what aligns with your personal values, and what you think you might enjoy.

There are many easy ways to incorporate skills learning into your daily life:

- Try cooking a new recipe.
- Consider taking on a different role at work.
- Embark on a DIY project at home.
- Start a new hobby like gardening or pottery.
- Take a course online.

Successive Approximation

A final guiding principle for building mastery is to increase the difficulty of your tasks and activities only when you feel ready. In other words, up the ante over time, and try to match the complexity of your behaviors to your current level of confidence.

It is important to be patient with yourself, and to give yourself time to build your skills and capabilities. Don't throw yourself straight into the deep end of a situation. Rather, work in the order laid out by this chapter: Start by doing things you have done before, then move on to challenging yourself with new experiences and skills.

A useful tool to ensure that you are taking things one step at a time is successive approximation. This strategy involves breaking up seemingly large and difficult tasks into small and accomplishable steps. Not only does this make bigger problems and goals seem less overwhelming, but it also allows you to map out a clear and actionable path to success.

Successive approximation is also relevant to activity scheduling and goal setting, but it is particularly helpful for building mastery because completing each step generates a renewed sense of capability. Based on your previous success, you are motivated for each next step, and by the end of the task, you would have built up a huge amount of confidence in yourself.

The Power of Positivity

As we learned earlier in this chapter, self-esteem is about how you see yourself and how you feel about yourself. A vitally important factor shaping this self-perception is how you talk to yourself.

Constantly talking down to yourself, and criticizing who you are and what you do, is a recipe for bad self-esteem. We saw in Chapter 7 how extensively our negative thoughts can impact our emotions and behaviors, so monitoring your own self-talk is essential for maintaining a good relationship with yourself.

One way to do this is by using the tools that we learned in Chapter 7. For example, positive thought replacement is an effective option for dealing with self-critical thoughts. As you notice them pop into your head, immediately try to replace this criticism by complimenting yourself instead.

Affirmations

You can also counter negativity by actively engaging in positive self-talk and daily affirmations. The goal of this technique is to use simple and positive self-statements to build yourself up. You can write these statements down in your journal, or say them out loud to yourself in the mirror.

Initially, you may not necessarily believe your affirmations, but remember that the point is more to transform your self-perception. Over time, practice will reinforce this new view of yourself, and you will find yourself identifying genuinely with your affirmations.

So, consider starting your day tomorrow with a positive self-statement:

- "I am confident, strong, and capable."
- "I am doing better every day."
- "Today, I will accomplish something new."

This kind of self-talk is also effective in a situational sense. For example, you can use positive statements to comfort or soothe yourself in a moment of distress, or to motivate yourself through goal setting and problem-solving.

Gratitude

In addition to positive affirmations and self-talk, you can also develop a gratitude practice to help change your self-perception. The goal of such a practice is simply to focus on the good things about yourself, and in your life, that you can be grateful for.

Gratitude is unique to everyone, so how you decide to carry out this practice is up to you. For example, you can incorporate gratitude into your journaling time by writing down something that you are grateful for at the beginning of each day. You could also add gratitude to your mindful meditation practices by focusing your awareness on the positive: your good physical health, a sense of contentment, or the beautiful surroundings.

Remember that nothing is too small to express gratitude over. Moreover, as you engage in this practice, your overall mindset will become more positive, and it will be easier for you to focus on the good.

Self-Compassion

Above all else, what underpins a positive self-perception is the concept of self-compassion. Having compassion for yourself is about learning to love and accept yourself as you are, and it is a vital foundational step toward building good self-esteem.

There are many different ways to practice having more compassion for yourself:

- Treat yourself with more kindness, and work on increasing your own sense of worth by practicing self-care (see Chapter 13 for more).
- Accept that no one is perfect, allow yourself to fail, and forgive yourself for your mistakes.
- Be mindful of your emotions, and don't let yourself become too overwhelmed or consumed by them.
- Stop comparing yourself to others, and remember that you don't have to live up to any standards except your own.
- Surround yourself with positive people, and set careful boundaries in your relationships to ensure that you are prioritizing those who build you up.

CHAPTER 12: INTERPERSONAL EFFECTIVENESS

So far, this book has dealt with a lot of intrapersonal techniques that are aimed at dealing specifically with your own thoughts, emotions, and actions. Anyone with mental health challenges will know how important these tools and strategies are, but they will also be aware of how having a mental health condition can affect the interpersonal aspects of their lives.

We do not live in a vacuum, and having stable and meaningful social relationships is important for maintaining good mental health. Often, our mental health struggles can make establishing and maintaining these connections more difficult, but there are several useful strategies for improving interpersonal effectiveness.

Social Creatures

Humans are social creatures who crave connection and companionship. We do not thrive in complete isolation, and we have emotional and interpersonal needs that we need to fulfill.

Additionally, there are a number of benefits to connecting with others and having good relationships with people. Interpersonal connection allows you to find and provide emotional support and companionship.

It gives you the opportunity to share positive experiences, and it helps you to build up your own sense of self-worth.

There are many general ways in which you can strengthen your relationships and connections:

- Take the opportunity to interact with others on a regular basis. For example, you can have lunch with your work colleagues instead of sitting alone.

- Socialize intentionally with friends and family whose company you enjoy. It is a good idea to make plans in advance, and to try to do something that everyone will find fun.

- Join a social or special interest group to network and interact with people who share similar interests to you.

- Help others by participating in volunteering work and community support organizations.

- Act with kindness when interacting with others. This can be as simple as saying thank you to someone who holds the door open for you.

- Talk to someone you trust about your feelings, and reciprocate this emotional support by being there for them in return.

Face Time

In this day and age, we do have the luxury of using technology to stay in touch with others, and it is great to be able to take advantage of these tools. But be cautious not to rely too much on social media to build and maintain your relationships. The risk is that you get into the habit of only ever texting and messaging, and you miss out on crucial face-to-face time with others.

You should try to prioritize face time in your relationships because this kind of interaction has a unique mood boosting quality. Socializing face-to-face allows us to work on our empathy, body language, and communication skills. Moreover, being able to see visual proof of your interaction with another person is important for validating that relationship, and it will only help to build a stronger connection.

Also keep in mind, however, that technology is not the absolute enemy in this regard. Video chat applications like Skype, Zoom, and FaceTime make it possible to overcome all kinds of obstacles to interpersonal interaction. This means that you don't have to let things like geographical distance or a global pandemic stop you from socializing with others.

Interpersonal Effectiveness

These general tips are useful for anyone wanting to improve their social skills and connections, but there are also specific tools for people who struggle more chronically with interpersonal relationships.

Interpersonal effectiveness is a cornerstone of DBT, and it is designed to help those who have difficulty with stability and communication in relationships. The rest of this chapter will be devoted to exploring these tools, and the focus of each technique is on how to communicate deliberately and thoughtfully rather than reactively and impulsively.

Overall, interpersonal effectiveness is about helping you to create healthy relationships while still taking care of yourself. It is about being able to ask for what you need, and to say no when necessary. The techniques below should also teach the skills of active listening and conflict resolution.

Each of these skills is tied to a different type of interpersonal effectiveness, so the skill set you choose to implement will depend on what kind of effectiveness you want to achieve in that situation.

Objective Effectiveness

Objective effectiveness is related to the purpose or goal of an interaction. It is about being able to accomplish a tangible or identifiable outcome.

So, if you have a specific goal in mind with regards to an interpersonal situation, you should practice implementing the objective effectiveness techniques: describe, express, assert, reinforce, mindfulness, appear confident, and negotiate (DEARMAN).

DEARMAN outlines the steps for assertive and effective communication. Its underlying idea is that you can increase the likelihood of your desired outcome by clearly expressing your needs and being respectful to all parties involved.

Describe

The first step of DEARMAN is to describe your situation clearly to the other person. Here, you should focus on the facts, avoid making any judgments, and simply explain how the issue appears to you personally.

For example, let's imagine that you want to talk to your boss about the problems you are having with their new schedule. Begin your DEARMAN exercise, and describe the issue clearly by saying something like, "You have put me on the new schedule to work the late shift every day this week."

Express

Your next step is to express your emotions and feelings about the situation. Try to use "I" statements to make it clear that you are explaining how the issue makes you feel.

For the above example, you could say to your boss, "I feel overwhelmed by the demands and pressure of the new schedule."

Assert

Next, assert your goals and wishes for the situation. For this step, you need to be very specific, and state exactly what you want by giving instructions or making requests. To do this effectively, you will need to know the outcome you want before going into the situation, so make sure that you have given a lot of prior thought to your desired result.

You can assert your goals with your boss by stating a specific alternative or solution to the current situation such as, "I need to work late only every second day of the week."

Reinforce

The next step of DEARMAN is about letting the other person respond to your assertions, and then engaging in positive reinforcement following their response. The best way to do this is by rewarding positive responses as this will reinforce the desirability of your outcome.

If your boss agrees to your assertions, positively reinforce this by smiling and thanking them.

Mindfulness

Throughout your use of DEARMAN, remember to stay present in the moment, and to remain focused on your goal. This means not getting distracted or sidetracked.

For example, don't bring up other issues while you have your boss's attention. Remember that you are there to discuss the new schedule, so don't ask for a pay raise while you're at it.

Appear Confident

DEARMAN also encourages you to appear confident throughout your interaction. Appearing confident is important for your own sense of capability. It will also make your desired outcome more likely because it shows the other person that you are clear and conscientious in your intentions. The best way to appear confident is to use open and self-assured body language, and to keep an upbeat, positive tone.

For example, when speaking with your boss, stand straight with your shoulders back, make consistent eye contact, and speak articulately and audibly.

Negotiate

The final step of DEARMAN is to remember that both parties in an interpersonal interaction will have valid feelings, motivations, and needs. As such, it is important to be willing to negotiate and compromise in order to resolve an issue. You need to be able to do this without disrespecting yourself, so make sure that you know your limits and boundaries going into the situation.

If your boss has not responded positively to your assertions, you could suggest a compromise like, "I will stick to your schedule for this week, but from next week, I won't be able to manage late shifts every day."

Relationship Effectiveness

Relationship effectiveness is about striving for conflict-free relationships through healthy interaction.

The strategies of this effectiveness can be implemented in situations where you want to resolve a conflict, or when you want to return to a less conflictual state with another person. These tools are a guide for harmonious communication, and they dictate that you should be gentle, interested, validating, and easy (GIVE) if you want to be successful.

Gentle

The first rule of the GIVE tool is to approach the other party in a nonthreatening and gentle manner.

This can be as simple as being nice and respectful to the other person, but it is also about avoiding harassment of any kind. This means not making any attacks, manipulation, or judgments. Moreover, be sure not to rely on words of anger or threats like, "I'll break up with you unless you do this for me."

Instead, try to stay calm and realistic when describing any painful and difficult emotions. Don't exaggerate or allow yourself to become overwhelmed. If you must take a break, ask the other party if you can pause the situation, and then step away until you have collected yourself.

Interested

GIVE states that it is also crucial to stay interested in the other party.

You can do this most effectively by using your body language. For example, indicate your interest by facing the other person head on, making consistent eye contact, and leaning slightly toward them.

You can also show your interest by actively listening to their point of view, and not interrupting them. Show that you are sensitive to their needs, and don't try to talk over them. Respect their wishes, even if this means waiting until they are more willing to engage with you.

Validating

The "V" in GIVE stands for validating, which means acknowledging the other person's opinions, needs, and feelings.

In order to resolve a conflict, it is important to be able to look at things from another's perspective, and to show that you understand their point of view. You can demonstrate this explicitly by saying something like, "I can hear that you are feeling frustrated."

Easy

The final rule of GIVE is to try to engage with an easy manner throughout the interaction.

This means leaving your attitude at the door, and staying positive and upbeat. For example, try to use an engaging tone, consider adding in some humor, and remember to smile.

While the conflict that you are trying to resolve may be serious, keeping the interaction lighthearted is more likely to reduce the tension between you and the other person.

Self-Respect Effectiveness

Self-respect effectiveness is about learning to maintain your boundaries, and to respect yourself throughout an interpersonal interaction.

The tools of this effectiveness aim to ensure that you do not feel disrespected in a relationship, and that you do not sacrifice your own values in order to please someone else. The guiding principles for achieving self-respect effectiveness are to be fair, apologize less, stick to your values, and be truthful (FAST).

Fair

The first rule of FAST is to be fair to yourself, as well as to the other person. Being fair to everyone involved in an interaction is the best way to avoid resentment in a relationship. It also allows you to give and receive constructive criticism.

You can practice fairness by being tactful and honest. This means carefully considering your own feelings, and reflecting on the emotions and opinions of the other party. You can then let these observations guide your actions, and the golden rule is to treat others how you would want them to treat you.

Apologize Less

The second rule of FAST is to apologize less. This means that you take responsibility only when appropriate, and apologize only when necessary.

The aim of this tool is to ensure that you are not overcompensating or feeling guilty without reason, and that you are not taking on responsibility that belongs to others.

Sticking To Your Values

FAST also highlights the importance of value engagement. Sticking to your values when interacting with others means not compromising your integrity for them.

In other words, you shouldn't sacrifice your beliefs, values, or boundaries in order to make someone else happy, or to resolve a conflict more quickly. In fact, staying true to who you are is exactly what will give you the confidence and self-esteem to resolve the issue most effectively.

Truthful

The final principle of FAST is about being truthful. This means avoiding lies, excuses, and exaggeration, and not acting helpless in order to manipulate others.

Instead, in order to maintain self-respect, you need to take responsibility for your actions and hold yourself accountable. To do this effectively, set aside time to reflect on your behavior in order to make sure that you are engaging with integrity and honesty.

CHAPTER 13: SELF-CARE

For this final chapter, we will return to focusing on our relationship with ourselves. All of the tools and techniques explored in this book will be important for helping you to feel good about yourself and your life, and a lot of these strategies can be summarized under the concept of self-care.

Self-care is about being able to live well, and to take good care of yourself both physically and emotionally. In addition to what you have already learned in previous chapters, there are several acts and habits that you can engage in each day that will help you to realize the power of self-care and routine.

What Does Self-Care Look Like?

Self-care is simply about taking the time to do whatever you need in order to live well. It is about focusing more consciously on yourself, and deliberately working to improve and maintain your mental and physical health.

The aim of self-care is to help you to manage your stress and regulate your emotional experience. It is also important for increasing your physical energy and lowering your risk of illness.

When considering how to implement self-care in your life, it is crucial to keep in mind that self-care looks different for everyone. The idea is to do whatever works for you as long as you are engaging in healthy and positive behaviors that add to your mental and physical health.

You should also remember that self-care is often a case of trial and error, and that it will most likely take time, practice, and experimentation to figure out which habits and acts are best for you.

To begin your self-care journey, you can start by setting up a routine around the ordinary, daily activities that make you feel good about yourself: making the bed every morning, maintaining personal hygiene habits, and getting enough sunlight and fresh air each day.

Feel Good Hormones

Another important way to practice self-care is by incorporating more physical activity in your life. There is a mountain of evidence to prove that exercise is good for both your physical and mental health.

Physically, exercise is important for maintaining a healthy body weight, building strong muscles and bones, increasing physical energy, and lowering your risk of chronic illness and disease. Moreover, exercise lowers your blood pressure, improves your cholesterol levels, boosts your immune system, and helps to regulate your sleep.

In addition to all of these physical benefits, exercise also has a number of emotional and mental health benefits. This is because any kind of physical activity causes our bodies to release hormones called endorphins. These are hormones that make us feel good by reducing feelings of stress, anxiety, and depression.

Moreover, exercise causes changes to the parts of our brains that regulate anxiety and stress. Over time, these areas become more sensitive to other "feel good" hormones like norepinephrine and serotonin.

Incorporating more exercise is also a gateway to improving your motivation and sense of purpose. This is because physical activity is an easy area of your life in which to set goals and challenges for yourself. And as we saw in Chapter 9, living with this kind of intention and meaning is essential for moving toward good mental health.

Move More

There are many different types of physical activity, but overall, exercise can be divided into two broad categories: cardio and strength exercise. Cardio activity, like running, cycling, and swimming, is aimed at improving your fitness and endurance. Strength exercises, like Pilates and weight training, are about building up your muscle strength and flexibility.

For the purposes of self-care, the basic idea is simply to move more. The best type of exercise for you will be whatever you most enjoy. You do not need to join a gym or take up a new sport. Rather, just choose something fun that you can stick to and incorporate easily into your existing routine.

You can choose your means of movement by considering which activities you already enjoy, and focusing on ones that involve physical activity: gardening, walking the dog, hiking, cleaning the house, stretching, or dancing.

Engaging in just 30 minutes of some kind of activity every day is enough to tap into the benefits of exercise mentioned above. Remember to be realistic in your intentions and goals, and don't be discouraged if it takes a while for you to work up to the full half hour of movement.

Eat, Sleep, Repeat

Eating Well

Another way to incorporate self-care into your daily life is to focus more consciously on what you are putting into your body. Eating well is important for physical health in the same way as exercise. Similarly, maintaining a balanced and healthy diet is essential for good mental health.

This is because what you eat directly affects your energy levels, focus, concentration, and mood. Healthy foods, like fruit, vegetables, and healthy fats, will positively affect these factors, while less healthy foods will have a more detrimental impact on your body and mind.

While moderation is important for all aspects of life, if you are wanting to eat well for your physical and mental health, you should consider limiting these less healthy foods: caffeine, sugar, alcohol, and anything fried, fatty, and salty.

Bedtime

It is also vital that you are prioritizing sleep as a means of self-care. Getting enough sleep is crucial for ensuring that your body and mind have time to rest, relax, and repair. As such, in order to be fully functioning and healthy adults, make sure that you are regularly getting between seven and nine hours of sleep each night.

If you are struggling with your sleeping routine, there are a few tips and tricks that you can try:

- Stick to a schedule by going to bed and waking up at the same time each and every day.
- Limit your blue light exposure close to bedtime by switching off phones and computer screens.
- Avoid alcohol and caffeine before bed.
- Establish a relaxing routine to help you wind down before bed. For example, reading for an hour, engaging in a meditation practice, or listening to a white noise machine.

Building Habits

Routine is not just an important part of sleeping well: The power of routine can be useful in all areas of life. This is primarily because, when we organize ourselves and our lives, we know what to expect and can more easily deal with stress and challenges.

Routine helps to make us feel grounded and safe, and we can implement regular habits in order to reap the benefits of this security.

It is also easier to engage in our self-care practices consistently when we have a fixed routine around things like exercising, eating, and sleeping.

The importance of having routine has also been specifically associated with positive benefits for those suffering from mental health conditions. This is because regularity and organization are foundational factors for being able to actively address symptoms and challenges.

The next section outlines a tool that can be useful in remembering the different habits that you should incorporate into your daily routine: accumulating positive experiences, building mastery, and coping ahead (ABC). This section also covers a tool that summarizes the components of self-care: treating physical illness, eating well, avoiding harmful substances, sleeping, and exercising (the PLEASE tool).

ABC PLEASE

The ABC PLEASE technique is an easy to remember acronym that includes several tools for how to take care of yourself. The overall aim of this skill is to reduce your physical and emotional vulnerability.

Accumulate

The first part of ABC is about accumulating positive emotions by doing fun and pleasant things.

This goes back to what we learned in Chapter 9 about the benefits of activity scheduling and behavior activation. Have another read of this chapter to remind yourself how you can use behavior and goal setting to motivate yourself, boost your mood, and live more consciously with purpose and meaning.

Build

The second part of ABC refers to the build mastery skill, which is designed to help you feel confident and capable and to boost your self-esteem.

Chapter 11 explores how to build mastery by doing what you enjoy, being open to new experiences, and learning new skills. Remember that the aim of building mastery is to establish a repertoire of behaviors that you find pleasant, and to build a wealth of evidence about your own abilities.

Cope

The "C" in ABC refers to the cope ahead tool. This is a technique that helps you to prepare for future events that are causing anxiety and stress.

You can head back to our discussion on coping ahead in Chapter 6 to see how this strategy is useful for emotional regulation and resilience. The aim of this tool is to reduce your emotional vulnerability and to stabilize your emotional experience.

PLEASE

The PLEASE skill serves as a reminder of the self-care techniques we have explored in this chapter, and it adds in a few more important rules for taking care of yourself:

- The first step of PLEASE is the "PL", which refers to treating physical illness. This means being responsible, and taking accountability for your health by visiting the doctor when you are sick, taking medications as prescribed, and allowing yourself to heal and rest when necessary.
- The "E" in PLEASE stands for eating, and this tool encourages eating a balanced diet in order to ensure mood stability.
- The "A" refers to avoiding mood alternating substances, similarly for the purposes of mood stability and control.
- The "S" refers to the importance of good sleep, which is explained in the previous section.
- Finally, the second "E" in PLEASE is for exercising to boost your mood, and to ensure the other benefits of physical activity as explored above.

CONCLUSION

Having arrived at the conclusion of this book, it should be absolutely clear to you that there are many different ways to deal with your mental health challenges.

While these strategies may take time, practice, and patience, they are also simple and easy to engage with. Another crucial takeaway is that these tools and techniques are all practical actions that you can implement in your daily life. The overall aim of this book has been to help you to help yourself.

Power and Worth

It is also important to remember that you hold the power to help yourself in this way.

Mental health challenges can often make us feel hopeless and incapacitated. We feel helpless in the face of our struggles, and become stuck in the mindset that there is no way out. We often do not believe that we can change, or that we are worthy of living differently.

But the truth is that managing mental illness is not impossible. You do not have to keep struggling as you do with overwhelming emotions, thoughts, and behaviors. You do not have to let your mental health condition affect your relationships and everyday functioning. There are, in fact, many solutions, and you have the power to put them into practice.

Change is possible. Even if you go slowly, and take it one step at a time, every bit of effort you put into actively working on yourself will make a difference. The key is to start somewhere, and to go from there.

A second important truth is that you deserve a full and happy life. Not only can you try to heal, but you should. Everyone is worthy of good mental health. You are not alone in your struggles and efforts, and you are just as entitled to healing, happiness, and health as everyone else.

Your Journey So Far

The great thing about having finished this book is that it means you have already taken the first step on your mental health journey.

Having knowledge of all of the tools and techniques available provides a solid foundation for you to put them into practice. You should know much more now than you did before, and to end off this book, here is a brief summary of the strategies you have learned:

- Chapter 3 taught you different distress tolerance techniques: TIPP, self-soothing, improving the moment, weighing the pros and cons, distraction, and radical acceptance.
- Chapter 4 was centered on mindfulness, and you would have learned the different mindfulness skills, as well as the steps to several meditation practices.
- If you are looking for more relaxation strategies, then you can head back to Chapter 5 for guidance on breathing techniques,

autogenic relaxation, progressive muscle relaxation, and visualization.

- Chapter 6 was all about emotional regulation, and it explored several useful tools for understanding and controlling your own emotions: STOP, identifying and labeling, the opposite action skill, and the cope ahead tool.

- The next chapter was similar in that it outlined techniques for addressing and influencing your own thoughts: fact-checking, cognitive restructuring, creating dysfunctional thought records, and cognitive reframing.

- Chapter 8 explored journaling, and it included many tools for self-reflection and self-monitoring: writing in free form, using writing prompts, the ABC model, activity, and mood tracking, and playing the script to the end.

- Chapter 9 delved more deeply into the ideas of motivation and purpose, and it explored techniques like activity scheduling, behavior activation, and goal setting.

- The next chapter on problem-solving aimed to help you deal with any challenges that might arise in the course of engaging with the tools of this book.

- Chapter 11 focused on helping you to improve your self-esteem and confidence using the build mastery tool, daily affirmations, gratitude practices, and self-compassion.

- Chapter 12 taught you about interpersonal effectiveness, and it explored several tools for creating healthy and communicative relationships: DEARMAN, GIVE, and FAST.
- Finally, Chapter 13 examined self-care. It encouraged you to exercise, eat and sleep well, and to maintain routine in order to care for yourself physically and emotionally. It also ended with a useful tool that summarized the self-care components and other skills of this book: ABC PLEASE.

Your next step, if you haven't already, is to start practicing.

There is no right or wrong way to implement these strategies in your life: Not all of these ideas will appeal to you, and that's okay. Take what speaks to you, what feels right, and what seems like a good fit, and leave the rest.

Above all, remember that you are capable and deserving of healing, happiness, and health.

References

Ackerman, C. E. (2017, March 20). CBT techniques: 25 cognitive behavioral therapy worksheets. Positive Psychology. https://positivepsychology.com/cbt-cognitive-behavioral-therapy-techniques-worksheets/

Ankrom, S. (2023, January 27). 9 breathing exercises to relieve anxiety. Very Well Mind. https://www.verywellmind.com/abdominal-breathing-2584115

Anonymous. (2017, July 31). What is cognitive behavioral therapy? https://www.apa.org/ptsd-guideline/patients-and-families/cognitive-behavioral

Anonymous. (2022, April 28). Relaxation techniques: Try these steps to reduce stress. https://www.mayoclinic.org/healthy-lifestyle/stress-management/in-depth/relaxation-technique/art-20045368

Anonymous. (2022, December 12). Borderline personality disorder. https://www.mayoclinic.org/diseases-conditions/borderline-personality-disorder/symptoms-causes/syc-20370237

Anonymous. (2022, December 16). 5 steps to mental wellbeing. https://www.nhs.uk/mental-health/self-help/guides-tools-and-activities/five-steps-to-mental-wellbeing/

Anonymous. (2022, June 8). Mental disorders. https://www.who.int/news-room/fact-sheets/detail/mental-disorders

Anonymous. (2022, October 11). Mindfulness exercises. https://www.mayoclinic.org/healthy-lifestyle/consumer-health/in-depth/mindfulness-exercises/art-20046356

Anonymous. (2022, September 29). Problem-solving. https://www.nhs.uk/every-mind-matters/mental-wellbeing-tips/self-help-cbt-techniques/problem-solving/

Anonymous. (n.d.). Caring for your mental health. https://www.nimh.nih.gov/health/topics/caring-for-your-mental-health

Anonymous. (n.d.). DBT skill: DEARMAN. https://www.therapistaid.com/therapy-worksheet/dbt-dear-man

Anonymous. (n.d.). Emotional regulation skills. https://dbt.tools/emotional_regulation/index.php

Anonymous. (n.d.). GIVE skill. https://dbt.tools/interpersonal_effectiveness/give.php

Anonymous. (n.d.). Mental Illness. https://www.nimh.nih.gov/health/statistics/mental-illness

Anonymous. (n.d.). Our best mental health tips—backed by research. https://www.mentalhealth.org.uk/explore-mental-health/publications/our-best-mental-health-tips

Anonymous. (n.d.). Personality disorders. https://www.nimh.nih.gov/health/statistics/personality-disorders

Arocho, J. (2015, November 23). How CBT uses goal setting. Manhattan Center for Cognitive Behavioral Therapy. https://www.manhattancbt.com/archives/544/cbt-uses-goal-setting/

Bray, S. (2013, April 16). Interpersonal effectiveness in dialectical behavior therapy. Good Therapy. https://www.goodtherapy.org/blog/interpersonal-effectiveness-dialectical-behavior-therapy-dbt-0416134

Chowdhury, M. R. (2019, August 13). Emotional regulation: 6 key skills to regulate emotions. Positive Psychology. https://positivepsychology.com/emotion-regulation/

Compitus, K. (2020, October 1). What are distress tolerance skills? Your ultimate DBT toolkit. Positive Psychology. https://positivepsychology.com/distress-tolerance-skills/

Cox, J. (2022, April 15). How to build your self-esteem. Psych Central. https://psychcentral.com/health/12-simple-activities-you-can-do-to-start-building-self-esteem-today

Holland, K. (2023, March 9). Mental health basics: types of mental illness, diagnosis, treatment, and more. Healthline. https://www.healthline.com/health/mental-health

Jones, S. M. W. (2022, February 2). Solving problems the cognitive–behavioral way. Psychology Today. https://www.psychologytoday.com/za/blog/all-about-cognitive-and-behavior-therapy/202202/solving-problems-the-cognitive-behavioral-way

Lindberg, S. (2019, November 2019). What to know about autogenic training. Healthline. https://www.healthline.com/health/mental-health/autogenic-training

Mairanz, A. (2017, September 18). Improve self-esteem and confidence by building mastery. Empower Your Mind Therapy. https://eymtherapy.com/blog/improve-self-esteem-and-confidence-by-building-mastery/

Moore, M. (2022, July 7). 4 DBT skills for everyday challenges. Psych Central. https://psychcentral.com/health/dbt-skills-therapy-techniques

Moore, M. (2022, June 23). Mindfulness: the art of cultivating resilience. Psych Central. https://psychcentral.com/lib/mindfulness-the-art-of-cultivating-resilience

Pitcher, S. (2020, June 17). DBT interpersonal skills: FAST. Nourish Your Mind. https://nourishyourmind.com/2020/06/dbt-interpersonal-skill-fast/

Plata, M. (2018, October 4). The power of routines in your mental health. Psychology Today. https://www.psychologytoday.com/za/blog/the-gen-y-psy/201810/the-power-of-routines-in-your-mental-health

Ragnarson, R. (2019, January 25). Cognitive journaling: a systematic method to overcome negative beliefs. Better Humans.

https://betterhumans.pub/cognitive-journaling-a-systematic-method-to-overcome-negative-beliefs-119be459842c

Roncero, A. (2021, June 21). Automatic negative thoughts: how to identify and fix them. Better Up. https://www.betterup.com/blog/automatic-thoughts

Semeco, A. (2023, February 9). The top 10 benefits to regular exercise. Healthline. https://www.healthline.com/nutrition/10-benefits-of-exercise

Smith, M., Robinson, L. & Segal, J. (2023, March 1). Building better mental health. Help Guide. https://www.helpguide.org/articles/mental-health/building-better-mental-health.htm

Stanborough, R. J. (2022, October 25). What are cognitive distortions and how can you change these thinking patterns? Healthline. https://www.healthline.com/health/cognitive-distortions

Tartakovsky, M. (2021, May 21). What is dialectical behavior therapy? Psych Central. https://psychcentral.com/lib/an-overview-of-dialectical-behavior-therapy

Villines, Z. (2021, October 24). What is behavioral activation? Medical News Today. https://www.medicalnewstoday.com/articles/behavioral-activation

Waichler, I. (2022, February 4). Activity scheduling: what it is, examples, and effectiveness. Choosing Therapy. https://www.choosingtherapy.com/activity-scheduling/

Made in the USA
Monee, IL
04 November 2026

67380044R00079